REASON TO BELIEVE

REASON TO BELIEVE
Romanticism, Pragmatism, and the Possibility of Teaching

Hephzibah Roskelly and Kate Ronald

STATE UNIVERSITY OF NEW YORK PRESS

Cover painting by Andrew Melrose, *Westward the Star of Empire Makes Its Way, Near Council Bluff Iowa*, circa 1865. Reproduced with permission of MIT Press.

Published by
State University of New York Press

© 1998 State University of New York Press

For information, address the State University of New York Press, State University Plaza, Albany, NY 12246

Production by Bernadine Dawes • Marketing by Fran Keneston

Library of Congress Cataloging-in-Publication Data

Roskelly, Hephzibah.
    Reason to believe : romanticism, pragmatism, and the possibility of teaching / Hephzibah Roskelly and Kate Ronald.
       p.   cm.
    Includes bibliographical references and index.
    ISBN 0-7914-3795-7 (hc : alk. paper). — ISBN 0-7914-3796-5 (pb : alk. paper)
       1. English language—Rhetoric—Study and teaching.
    2. Romanticism. 3. Pragmatism. I. Ronald, Kate. II. Title.
PE1404.R67   1998
808'.042'071—dc21   97-44192
                                                  CIP

1 2 3 4 5 6 7 8 9 10

For
Ann Berthoff
and
Dottie Broaddus
and
in memory of Paulo Freire

Contents

Acknowledgments

We are grateful to Beatrice Butell Vaughn-Bayer for being such a knowledgeable guide on our visit to the Old Manse and for allowing us to visit the attic room.

We would like to thank Laura Harping for generously reading and carefully editing this manuscript. Our thanks go as well to Andrew McCuaig, Pegeen Reichert-Powell, Sidelia Reyna, and Faydra Womble for their help in proofreading, and to David Prout for his skillful indexing.

We also want to thank those teachers and students who allowed us into their classrooms, who graciously permitted us to use their words, and whose work represents for us the best kind of romantic/pragmatic rhetoric: Bill Buczinsky, Thomas Riddle, Marsha Holmes, Chris Bachelder, Evan Post, Beth Rendell, and Philip Haigh.

Preface

At the end of every hard-earned day, people find some reason to believe.

—Bruce Springsteen

We have begun this book many times, but its true beginning came in an attic, and the story of that attic represents for us the impulses behind as well as the goals for *Reason to Believe*. The attic sits atop the Old Manse, Ralph Waldo Emerson's family home in Concord, Massachusetts, open to the public for tours. Several years ago, we were in Boston, doing research on romantic rhetoric and pragmatism for this project at Harvard's Widener Library. We were with our dear friend and one of the most pragmatic romantics we know, Dottie Broaddus. Needing a break, and being good romantics, we went to the country, specifically to Concord. We'd been there before, several times, and had walked over the "rude bridge" where the "shot heard round the world" marked the beginning of the Revolutionary War. We'd been to Louisa May Alcott's house, we'd walked around Walden, and we'd visited Sleepy Hollow Cemetery, where Emerson, Thoreau, Hawthorne, Fuller, and the Alcotts had walked and talked and now were buried.

We had also been before to the Old Manse, Emerson's family's frequent home and the place where Hawthorne spent three years of the honeymoon that was his marriage. But we went back that magical Sunday. And we took the tour again. We saw where Sophia and Nathaniel had scratched "Man's accidents are God's purposes" in the windowpane in the second-floor study after her miscarriage. We saw the bed they painted yellow in their bedroom, which they called "the golden world." And we looked at the desk where Emerson and his father and grandfather composed their sermons. We browsed through the books they read there, annoying our guide, who kept admonishing us to move on. (They don't let you wander; in fact they keep a very close eye on you and hurry you through.) But we were satisfied. We even felt inspired about our book, imagining all the talk about belief and possibility that these walls had heard.

And then the guide told the group, almost in an aside, that Emerson had carved some sayings in the wood around the fireplace in a bedroom in the attic, where he used to stay when he came to preach and to write. We looked at each other, at the door to the attic marked "Not open to the public," then more slyly back at each other. We felt more inspired—and determined to get up there.

The tour ended in the kitchen, and we lingered to talk to the woman who ran the Old Manse preservation project. We told her about *our* project, and Dottie (who also writes about the legacies of nineteenth-century men for twentieth-century education and culture) began asking her for the exact dates that Emerson had stayed in the house, so that we could figure out what exactly he might have composed there. The curator loved the idea that we knew something about him, and went for her notes. Then Hepsie asked her what Emerson had written on the walls upstairs. She couldn't remember; in fact, she thought maybe it wasn't Emerson at all, that perhaps it was his grandfather, or maybe his son. Kate said, "Well, why don't we go up and see?" For just a moment the guide's face took on that official "Tsk, tsk/Oh no, impossible" look. Then she paused for a long moment. Finally, she cocked her head and out of slitted, almost-twinkling eyes, said, "Do you all want to go up there with me and see what's written there?"

The next minute we were following her up two flights of steps while another tour was getting a glimpse of Hawthorne's favorite chair. We climbed up and into another, very narrow stairway that felt more like a ladder. In file behind her flashlight beam, we entered a tiny room with a wrought iron bed, a white spread, a writing table, and a fireplace. In the light of her lamp, we read and copied what can only be called graffiti from several generations of Emersons—Ralph Waldo Emerson's grandfather, his father, and perhaps his aunt Mary Moody. One had written:

> Holy and happy stand
> In consecrated gown

> Toil till some angel hand
> Bring sleep and shroud and crown.

Another had added:

> Peace to the soul of the blessed dead;
> Honor to the ambition of the living.

And finally, in Emerson's spidery script and signed with his initials, we read:

> I visited this room and read the inscription of the souls gone before.

It may not seem like much in the retelling. But as we stood there in the Old Manse attic, surrounded by private words on a wall that was now made public, and by past generations acknowledging their connection to their past and their present, we recognized something about our impulse to write this book.

We wanted, we realized, to do as Emerson had done when he looked at his grandfather's words and those others, against his own. How does the history of our thinking about education and learning and spiritual understanding in this country, a history bound up with people like those who lived in the Old Manse, connect to the works of teachers now? In exploring the worlds of the romantic and pragmatic philosophers of the American past, we show them to be living in the words of writers today. Gerda Lerner, historian and pioneer in women's history, writes in her latest book *Why History Matters* about the importance of historical study in this context:

> We learn from our construction of the past what possibilities and choices once existed. Assuming, as Henri Pirenne says, that the actions of the living and those of the dead are comparable, we then draw conclusions about the consequences of our present-day choices. This, in turn, enables us to project a vision of the future. It is through history-making that the present is freed from necessity and the past becomes usable. (1997, 117)

A past one can use and a present one can shape can lead, as Lerner argues, to a sense of possibility in a future, as history uncovers the connections between individuals and communities over time and space. When Emerson writes on the wall that he has read and understood the inscription of the "souls gone before," he acknowledges the human link that permits an understanding transcending and affirming individual history. And Ann Berthoff, our contemporary Concord mentor, demonstrates her understanding of a "usable past" when she writes that in interpretation "elements of what we want to end with must be present in some form from the first; otherwise, we will never get to them" (1982, 3). That statement is a pragmatic maxim, as all of her maxims are, because it insists that actions and beliefs entail one another, and that past and future become usable and possible when connected. In an academic culture where teachers' days seem, if not numbered exactly, at least increasingly hard-earned, the future may seem bleak and the past irrelevant. Lerner's project, Emerson's ambition, and Berthoff's design are to understand the story of the past and of the present as mutually reinforcing, and to find in both stories a reason to believe.

ONE

IS TEACHING STILL POSSIBLE?

> That species-specific capacity for thinking about thinking, for interpreting interpretations, for knowing our knowledge, is, I think, the chief resource for any teacher and the ground of hope in the enterprise of teaching reading and writing.
>
> —Ann Berthoff, "Is Teaching Still Possible?"

> There is no change without dream, as there is no dream without hope. . . . What kind of educator would I be if I did not feel moved by a powerful impulse to seek, without lying, convincing arguments in defense of the dreams for which I struggle, in defense of the "why" of the hope with which I act as an educator?
>
> —Paulo Freire, *Pedagogy of Hope*

We begin this book with a very big question because we are interested in the larger issues within the life of composition studies and the lives of composition teachers and students. *Reason to Believe* is both a historical account of a movement in rhetorical theory and philosophy that composition as a discipline has overlooked and an argument for why there can, indeed, be reasons to believe in the larger purposes and immediate usefulness of the work of teaching writing. To preview the following pages very briefly, in this book we suggest that composition, and English studies in general, can benefit from taking a new look at both American romanticism and pragmatism in order to revitalize itself, to reinvigorate its work with the sense of hope, mission, and passion that has been one of its hallmarks during the last thirty years— the belief in the power of language and in students' abilities to produce it. That belief seems to us lost, or at least hidden, gone underground in the current "social turn" in composition and the move to postmodern critical theory in English studies. One result has been the almost total dismissal and/or neglect of romantic influences on rhetorical theory and practice even though, as we will argue, what's best about philosophical romanticism is practically essential to any classroom teacher who wants to keep his or her teaching alive year after year.

Another result has been the privileging of what Cornel West calls "grand theory" over pedagogical practice, with the "process" revolution in composition superseded by "postprocess" theorizing that rarely speaks to classroom contexts and actual students. We are not suggesting that teachers choose theory or practice. On the contrary, the cynicism that results from pitting theory against practice can lead to a pedagogical and scholarly crisis of the spirit, a poverty of belief more damaging to the cause of real literacy than economic deprivation. We believe that theory and practice do connect, and must, if we're to continue to maintain that teaching is still possible. If Stanley Fish is right that there is "no direct causal relationship between one's account of one's practice and the actual shape of that practice" (1989, 362), we assert that he is wrong in believing that direct cause and effect is the only kind of relationship that theory and practice might maintain. What we will call romantic/pragmatic rhetoric, the philosophical practice that this book describes and traces, points to those other kinds of relationships and distinguishes them from the kind of "neopragmatism" that Fish advocates.

Neither are we suggesting a nostalgic or retrograde look backward to better times; rather, we point to a philosophical strand in the history of rhetoric and composition that has continued without the benefit of careful investigation, a theoretical position that has been forgotten in what Stephen North calls the "methodological land rush" to stake out territory for scholarship and legitimacy in composition (1987, 2). Locating in American romantic thought and its descendant pragmatism a philosophical position that suggests how theories might talk to one another and to teachers' and students' lived experience in and out of the classroom, this book suggests a romantic/pragmatic rhetoric that will make room for *belief,* not blind faith, in the work that teachers, writers, and students do everyday.

Ann Berthoff's question—"Is teaching still possible?"—may seem purely rhetorical. Throughout her work, she has continually challenged teachers to make teaching possible by reflecting on their own practices in order to unite theory and method. And so her question feels less like a query than an exhortation, a reminder to teachers to "keep the faith," to find, in what Berthoff calls "thinking about thinking," a reason to believe in their work. In her 1984 article, Berthoff argues that this consciousness of the mind at work, this "interpretation of interpretations," is the "chief resource for any teacher and the ground of hope in the enterprise of teaching reading and writing" (1984, 743). But Berthoff's question can also be read as a warning about the consequences of unexamined practice and a summons to the kind of reflection that sustainable belief requires.

Teachers who do not know the roots of their own beliefs and methods cannot act as persuasively as they might if they recognized their connections to a richly complicated past and examined how that past is used in current contexts. When teachers examine history in this way, both globally and locally, the stories they tell give them a new vocabulary of what Paulo Freire calls generative words, words that powerfully construct and deconstruct past, present, and future. Freire describes such words as basic to being and acting: "To exist, humanly, is to name the world, to change it. Once named, the world in its turn reappears to the namers as a problem and requires of them a new naming" (1970, 77). For most of recent pedagogical history, teachers have not been able to name—and so claim—a philosophy that embraces both idealism and practicalism, individuality and social responsibility, inquiry and faith. To examine the history of romanticism and pragmatism—to put them together as *romantic/pragmatic rhetoric*—is to recover a history and philosophy that teachers can use to question their own practices and beliefs and to give them theoretical support for the beliefs they continue to hold.

Without this historical and philosophical framework, teachers can easily become weary, cynical, or naive about theory's connection to their lived experiences in the classroom. Three of the most influential theorists in literary studies, composition, and Writing Centers, for example, have recently described what amounts to their own loss of faith in the connection, retreating into an odd mixture of cynicism and nostalgia. Jane Tompkins's "Pedagogy of the Distressed" acted as a sort of tonic to tired teachers in 1990. Tompkins began her essay by insisting that teachers always "preach some gospel or another. We do this indirectly," she says, "but always" (1990, 653). The frustration and the exhaustion she felt about her teaching came, she explains, because her practice didn't "come very close to instantiating the values" she preached (653). In other words, she wasn't really preaching, but doing what she calls "performing," showing her students how much she knew, hoping they would "think highly" of her intellect, and holding her students to the same ideal of performance in their work for her.

Tompkins's "pedagogy of the distressed" is a remarkable confession and conversion story. Tired of operating out of "fear," both of being exposed as knowing less than presumed and fear of teaching in general, at least talking about teaching or taking it seriously, Tompkins changes her classroom to a place that operates more out of her sense of "the way life ought to be" (657). She continues to write the syllabus for her classes, drawing on her own knowledge and expertise, but she turns the class work and class time over to the students, who present the material, debate, argue, and generally set the agendas and figure out the paths they want to take through Tompkins's courses. She describes one of the first courses she organized this way as "the best class I've never taught" (658). Tompkins completes her conversion narrative by announcing that "I can never teach in the old way again" and by offering a list of suggestions for "letting go" and "trusting the students" that mirror many of the writing process and workshop strategies that compositionists have been advocating for years.

Tompkins's student-centered pedagogy was not news in 1990, but her confession prompted a lot of discussion and soul-searching among *College English* readers. This article became a rallying cry for the examination of the material and emotional conditions of teachers across the country. Although she was accused of both elitism and romanticism (Tompkins's material conditions include Duke University and a full professorship, and she herself admitted that her suggestions may sound "utopian and childlike"), Tompkins countered that teachers must act to "draw energy" from students rather than "expend" it in order to avoid "burn out" and exhaustion (1991, 604).

The commotion over this article is more noteworthy than its suggestions for reform, and the themes that dominated discussions about it can shed light on Berthoff's question about the possibility of teaching. Tompkins emphasizes two dominant impediments to "life the way it ought to be": fear of exposure as a "fraud" and disdain for the pedagogical enterprise in the first place. These two reactions to teaching represent related strains in current thinking in the profession, both of which can lead to cynicism: teachers often operate out of "romantic" notions about their relationships with students and their roles in changing lives. When reality does not bear out these romantic dreams, teachers like Tompkins begin to question what they have to offer to students. Other teachers resort to "expediency," doing what's necessary to satisfy colleagues, administrators, school boards, principals, testing agencies, without thinking very much any more about the lofty goals for change and growth that perhaps led them to the classroom in the first place. These reactions, what we're going to call "mere" romanticism and "mere" expedience, are perfectly understandable given the material conditions for teachers in the late twentieth century. Tompkins admits that her overriding problem, the cause of her distress, was the sheer exhausting work of teaching. And her list of suggestions adds up, fundamentally, to ways to lighten her own burden. Teaching is tiresome, "empty labor which will end by killing the organism that engages in it" unless teachers find some way to make teaching "serve" them (1990, 660). Tompkins finds that way by "seeking rest" in a student-centered pedagogy, a move from what she calls the "performance" model to teaching as a "maternal or coaching" activity (660), so that the goal for trying new methods is not so much to nurture students' literacy development as to save teachers' sanity.

"Pedagogy of the Distressed" finally offers the mere romanticism of teacher as exhausted caretaker and the mere expedience of teacher as time-server. Starkly missing here is any theoretical foundation for or critical exploration of the methods Tompkins advocates, a striking omission from a writer who is known as a theorist. Her only nod to theory or ideology is in one, rather offhand sentence: "You might say I made the move in order to democratize the classroom" (660). Then, without any exploration of the term "democracy," she quickly concludes by saying that "on a practical plane I did it because I was tired" (660). Tompkins's answer to Berthoff's question, then, is ultimately cynical: teaching is possible if teachers find ways of escaping its work.

Five years later, Susan Miller returns to Tompkins's "distress" and uses it as a way into her own discussion of whether teaching is still possible . "The Death of the Teacher" casts doubt on the possibility of even speaking "about relationships between student and teacher"; Miller's theme is that the "Teacher, erstwhile Author of class(es), has expired" (1995, 42). In a complicated theoretical/historical overview, Miller argues that the postmodern teacher cannot adopt the historical role of Father, the "good man" that Cicero and Quintilian advocated, the doting parent, lover of students, and authority, the author of "conduct books on Western patriarchy," who initiates students into the power structures already in place (42). Neither can a teacher in good conscience embrace the managerial role of Mother, who "invades" students' lives by getting personal, who becomes a "feminized martyr," and whose job is to manage students' Otherness in ways that prove most "useful" to the culture that these Mothers inhabit and sustain. Miller cites the current explosion of work around issues of authority and the construction of authority as proof that, having rejected both these roles, "we have no stable way . . . to imagine a purpose for teaching" (49).

Miller ends her obituary of the teacher with a teacher's story about getting "relational," rather than "personal," in the public space that is her classroom. Her point seems to be that students are very different from you and me, and we'd best acknowledge that fact by accepting the death of what she calls "*the* teacher" and being simply another human being with our students. It's difficult to tell if Miller is advocating mere expediency; her emphasis on theoretical justifications for teachers' vocations suggests that she is not interested in accommodating to the systems in which she works. Finally, though, Miller leaves distressed teachers, who may be as tired as Tompkins was, with no real suggestions for relief or change. Like Tompkins, she describes her classes as student-focused places where the students "teach" and "act relationally" (50). She adds that she does not know if "this relationship approach works. I undertake it to attempt a theoretized admission of my differences from classes and my expectation that they will write, not merely read, discourses I may not join" (51). Although she denigrates Tompkins's epiphany and renewed commitment to teaching the "ideals we cherish," Miller finally offers only her own ephemeral story, with vague and elitist references to postmodern theory, to teachers who might have some hope of rising from the dead, or at least of sustaining some faith in their work. Where Tompkins advocates getting closer to students, forming a community of co-learners with them, Miller warns that such a community is a myth, and a dangerous one.

Neither Miller nor Tompkins, then, offers much reason for teachers to believe. Tompkins offers a practical suggestion for easing off, closing the door, and letting go of the burden of authority. But, as teachers who wrote back to *College English* after this article appeared argued, isolationism does not work for all teachers, most of whom are in decidedly less comfortable situations than Tompkins (see Carroll

1991). Besides, Tompkins's practical suggestions do not address the complicated and varied scenes of writing instruction or the very real theoretical issues about whose agendas are served in those settings. Miller, who seems caught completely in those theoretical agendas and without any suggestions for teachers, seems simply hopeless.

These two teachers can, for our purposes, represent the two extremes of talk about teaching—one "theoretical" and the other "practical." Despite composition's insistence that theory/practice cannot be separated, and its repeated attempts to relate theory and practice, these two terms remain opposed in a hierarchy that places theory above and practice below. Teachers remain, in Tompkins's and Miller's words, "tired," "frustrated," nagged by "fear," "dis-ease," and "guilt" because theory and practice have not been questioned in the ways Berthoff insists upon. Moreover, the convenient collapsing of theory/practice into one term masks dualistic assumptions about teaching writing and hides fundamental conflicts that keep teachers, not only *not* comfortable, but downright distressed. Both Miller and Tompkins attempt to expose some of those conflicts, by justifying practice theoretically, as Miller does, or by theorizing long-standing practices, as Tompkins suggests. But without a clear understanding of the historical nature of practice and philosophy, such arguments leave teachers with limited options: embrace the latest method, cling to nostalgic myths, believe in mythical promises, or keep doing what "works" in the classroom without questioning too much why. None of these options provides much hope.

One final example will serve to illustrate our belief that teachers need some way out of the theory/practice disjunction if they want to avoid this kind of retreat. This example comes from the literature on Writing Centers, where, because of Writing Centers' almost endemic marginal status within institutions and within composition itself, hope has been essential to the work of teachers and administrators. Hope—in students' abilities; in teachers' abilities to read, respond, think on their feet, challenge both students and colleagues; in possibilities for change within individuals and institutions—has often been difficult for Writing Centers to sustain, but without it, such Centers are left with only others' hopes, ideals, and agendas.

Yet we see a troubling move away from hope by one of the most influential teachers and theorists in Writing Center scholarship. Stephen North's "Revisiting 'The Idea of a Writing Center,'" written

ten years after his original "The Idea of a Writing Center," reveals a turn from hope to hopelessness, from faith to doubt, from large visions to narrow agendas. Both articles offer visions of Writing Centers, and this drive toward statements of principles and definitions is understandable in a branch of composition whose existence is most often described in expedient terms. Ironically, North moves from resisting an expedient concept of Writing Centers as the repair shops of the University to embracing an even narrower brand of expediency.

In 1984, North's "The Idea of a Writing Center" became a beacon of hope for Writing Centers nationally. North began that essay with a clever rhetorical move, claiming that he was addressing his essay to those "not involved" in Writing Centers, particularly to those, in English, who claim to "know" Writing Centers but who clearly do not. Then, in words directed to those deeply involved in Writing Centers, North describes his Writing Center at SUNY-Albany as a place open to all members of the University community and a site for dealing with whole pieces of discourse. A large portion of this essay was taken up with North's frustration over the University community's assumptions that the Writing Center is a place to "clean up" papers, often at the last minute, a place to send "impossible" students. North says that all the models for Writing Centers that frustrated him—"the grammar and drill center, the fix-it shop, the first-aid station"—are "vital and authentic reflections of a way of thinking about writing and the teaching of writing that is alive and well and living in English departments everywhere" (1984, 437). North wanted to change that reflection, change the mirror everyone, those involved and not involved, looked in when they looked at Writing Centers. He suggested, first of all, the privileging of writers over texts as the single distinguishing characteristic of his Writing Center (and by extension, all "good" Writing Centers). Texts are simply occasions for addressing processes, and writers and Writing Center teachers are participant-observers, participating and intervening in the rituals of writing.

North's own rhetorical stance is interesting here: as the administrator of this program, he claims a "hard, not conciliatory position": he, in fact, tells his assumed audience to get out of his face, for "teachers do not need, and cannot use, a writing center; only writers need it; only writers can use it. In short, we are not here to serve, supplement, back up, complement, reinforce or otherwise be defined by any external curriculum. . . . We are here to talk to writers." North ends his

stirring description of what Writing Centers should be by acknowledging that in order to "talk to writers," Centers may have to accommodate to institutional demands for credit-hour production, grammar hot
lines, faculty development. He admits that such expedient efforts "have
about them an air of shrewdness, or desperation, the trace of a survival
instinct at work" (446). But he also argues that ideally such "pragmatic"
moves may eventually help Writing Centers become the centers of
consciousness about writing on campuses, a kind of physical locus for
the ideas and ideals of college or university or high school commitment to writing (446). Heady stuff, and it gets even more so as North
insists "but not this way, not via the back door, not—like some marginal ballplayer—by doing whatever it takes to stay on the team. If
writing centers are going to finally be accepted, surely they must be
accepted on their own terms, as places whose primary responsibility,
whose only reason for being, is to talk to writers" (446). North ends
what he would later come to call this "romantic" vision by invoking
the "heritage" of Writing Centers in Socrates' methods of education.

In 1994, North "revisited" his earlier "Idea of a Writing Center,"
this time looking at his earlier vision as "attractive, in its own way,"
but also this time seeing his original principles as "a romantic idealization" that "presents its own kind of jeopardy" (1994, 9). He says his
earlier vision has "come back to haunt *us*," since this "reflection" of
Writing Centers has dominated composition's visions, not only of
Writing Centers but of the composition classroom (9; our emphasis).
Now North wants to take another look at that reflection. He takes
four passages from this 1984 article, four of his earlier "ideas," and
rereads them from the vantage point of ten years of work in his Writing Center, reimagining the scene of writing in the Center, not as a
place where motivated, eager "wrestlers" with texts come to find a
reader and multiple readings, but as a place where there are too many
students, with too many particular, different agendas, who have come
to the Center for all sorts of reasons, some merely expedient, and
who, simply, are too disruptive to his original vision to handle. As a
result, North substitutes one "ideal" Writing Center for another.

In other words, North's hope has become hopelessness. He refers
to his earlier goals for Writing Centers several times as "laughable"
(14). He replaces his four earlier ideas (that students come to the Center for their own purposes, that the Center's setting is safe, that the
Writing Center teacher and the classroom teacher can work from

mutual purposes, and that the Writing Center should be a center of consciousness about writing for the institution) with four new tenets for his Writing Center: (1) he'll have motivated students because he's only working with self-selected students enrolled in a "coherent four-year sequence of study," and not self-selected in terms of having the nerve to walk through the door of the Writing Center; (2) he'll have students there for sustained periods of time, because he's tired of the chaos and disruption of seeing so many people, sometimes only for one or two meetings; (3) he'll work within a "tighter orbit" of (again) self-selected faculty; he does not want to sustain a delicately balanced relationship with faculty; he wants only to deal with those like himself; (4) his new Writing Center will be tied to the Writing Sequence and English major, for ten faculty, twenty graduate students, and two hundred fifty undergraduates "that we can actually, sanely, responsibly bring together" (17). In favor of this narrowed vision, North rejects his earlier belief that a Writing Center could serve as a conscience about writing for the entire university. Indeed, this new vision narrows everything—the number and kind of students in the Writing Center, along with its methods and its goals.

North sounds tired in this latest article, which is understandable; all of us who have been doing this work through the 1980s and 1990s are tired. Increasing demands to account for and assess the work of teaching, decreasing budgets and increasing class sizes, and the growing doubt that teaching matters much in the overall institutional scheme can make anybody weary. North worries over the "fate" of the "truly talented, truly in-tune, truly committed English teacher—indeed, the litmus test of that commitment—is a kind of institutional martyrdom" (18). To resist that kind of exhausting martyrdom, North counsels retreat, the "crucial move—albeit a hard-nosed one"—into specialization, toward lessening his own martyrdom and his own burden by controlling his immediate environment, by choosing with whom he will talk about writing (18).

Although by his own rhetoric he tries to cast himself as a realist, North has replaced one sort of idealism with another. As he repudiates his former "romantic" notions of what a Writing Center could be, he reveals his own cynicism while replacing with a pragmatic method what he sees as a romantic dream. His movement away from belief comes out of his restlessness and frustration over being misunderstood, overworked, and undervalued, and it leads him to cast off and deny roles that previously seemed revolutionary, finally circling his wagons, and retreating into his own "expediency" and "merely" theoretical agendas that serve a smaller world. North's "idea of a Writing Center" has moved from global to local, and finally becomes *his* idea of *his* Writing Center. If there is any advice left for teachers in other places, it is to get "hard-nosed" themselves.

This move may not be surprising given North's desires, in both his "ideas," to settle the matter once and for all, to make a public statement about the work he will do, and the work he thinks his Writing Center is able to do. That desire is consistent with North's first public statement to composition, his *The Making of Knowledge in Composition*. This overview of the field, an admirable attempt to make sense of competing theories and to claim legitimacy for an emerging discipline, in fact was rigid in its categorization. This book institutionalized categories of knowledge into a taxonomy where philosophers, experimenters, scholars, historians, and researchers were cast in mutually exclusive positions and where none of this theoretical, research-oriented work connected to the last category North named, the teacher-"practitioner," who is left only with "lore" (1987, 23). If practitioners cannot effect change in the ways theory and knowledge are made, and if theory is unconnected to the work of the classroom, then it's no wonder that North ends up sounding cynical and despairing, making fun of his earlier hope, his lost, large vision.

North's most recent article does not offer any real look at the work of the teachers or students in the Writing Center. North "wrestles" with competing theories of teaching, comparing conflicting views of what constitutes worthy or valid work for a teacher of writing. North uses the latest and most "cutting edge" theory to defend a "timely" and "radical" restructuring of the material conditions in which he works, because the work is difficult and goes unrewarded in academic institutions. In the process, he risks losing sight of the rich and complicated history, experience, and lore of Writing Centers. He clearly needs to reduce his workload and elevate his status, and he calls upon theory to help him make these changes, but this theory/practice relationship works in only one way. If theory is not tested against practitioner knowledge and history, against student experience, if theories only compete with one another for dominance and never negotiate with practical "lore," then the kind of thinking about thinking that Berthoff calls for doesn't seem rigorous. Examining the consequences of ideas for action, asking who's being served by new theory or "restructuring" might also be considered "romantic" idealism, and romanticism is certainly something North wants to avoid in his revised, diminished vision of retreat.

This notion of retreat is precisely what George Will decries in a July 1995 *Washington Post* column that places the theory/practice academic debate squarely into its public and political context. In a commentary on an article in the quarterly *Public Interest* that raises the ancient question of "Why Johnny Can't Write," Will berates teachers of writing for abandoning the idea of "transmitting" anything to students and instead adhering to what he has heard called the "growth model" of teaching composition. He characterizes current writing teachers as "celebrating inarticulateness and error as proof of authenticity," and he lays the blame on "liberationist zeal, deconstructionist nihilism, and multicultural proselytizing." Will describes U.S. teachers as "refusing" to teach writing, choosing instead to teach a "workshop on racial and sexual oppression." Will's indictment is scathing: his own rhetoric is polar, casting process against content, personality against standards and chastising teachers for forcing students to "learn how language silences women and blacks" rather than "studying possessive pronouns" (1996, C7).

We don't take Will's alarmist rhetoric all that seriously, but he clearly has a large public audience, and his arguments, tiresomely familiar to composition theorists and directors, will need to be answered once again. His column is interesting for our purposes, though, in several ways. First, it's an apt example of how theory and practice are often viewed as polar opposites, how even practicing writers might believe that writing students need to study *either* grammar or "content." Quoting his source Heather McDonald's critique, Will writes, "Rather than studying possessive pronouns, students are learning how language silences women and blacks." Will's clear assumption that "studying possessive pronouns" is a neutral pedagogical activity and one more important than learning cultural history shows how prevalent the dualistic line of thinking remains. (And the unconsciously ironic connection between "possession" and women and blacks shows how prevalent racist and sexist lines of thinking remain.) Finally, Will's conclusion, where he describes the "smugly self-absorbed professoriate" as "often tenured and always comfortable" puts teacher and student in direct opposition as he contrasts them (us) with their (our) students, who are "always cheated and often unemployable" (C7). Obviously Will has not been in a composition classroom since his undergraduate days; clearly he has not read of Tompkins's "distress" or Miller's "relational" pedagogy. But however far off his description of academia might be, it recognizes the hostility of the public toward university professors who focus less on their teaching than on their research and the frustration of many teachers, who read in the results of that research a silence, or an arrogance, about the classroom and the enterprise of teaching itself.

One of the implications we read in Will's column is that a real answer to Berthoff's question might indeed be required, from teachers themselves, from their practices in their classrooms, from the administrative systems in which they work, from the public they serve, and, despite Will's bemoaning of its influence, from theory, which has changed and challenged traditional ways of thinking about the pedagogical enterprise. What's required, in Berthoff's terms, and what critics like Will neglect to do, is some genuine "thinking about thinking." The interpretive turn Berthoff would encourage demands that a theory embrace consequences and that practice acknowledge theoretical agendas, influences, alternatives.

Among all these writers, three of them insiders and one an "outsider" to academics, there is a sense of diminished hope and a retreat from action, a sense of how to name problems but no vocabulary for naming solutions as constructed within contexts that are at once philosophical, historical and local. Paulo Freire might characterize this retreat as the inevitable result of naive hope in the first place. In *A Pedagogy of Hope,* Freire says that

> The idea that hope alone will transform the world, and action undertaken in that kind of naiveté, is an excellent route to hopelessness. But the attempt to do without hope, in the struggle to improve the world, as if that struggle could be reduced to calculated acts alone, or a purely scientific approach, is a frivolous illusion. (1994, 8)

North's new Writing Center design is a "calculated act," calculated, like Tompkins's new classroom, to reduce stress, lighten the workload, and redefine the vocation of a teacher and an intellectual. Unlike Tompkins, North has lost most of his earlier hope; there's little fire in his revised vision, and he has abandoned what Freire argues are the two necessary conditions for hope: "rage and love, without which there is no hope" (10). We suggest that, in losing his rage, North has lost a lot of his hope.

North, Miller, Tompkins, and Will each offer some prevailing views of the teacher, and taken together they represent at least a range of possible roles for teachers of writing, a variety of answers to the question of whether teaching is still possible. Each of them, however, answers that question with a lessened sense of hope, a smaller definition of community, and limited possibilities for action. Cornel West, historian and philosopher, argues in *Keeping Faith* that "the lives of many academic intellectuals are characterized by *demoralization, marginalization, and irrelevance*" (1993a, 95). West devotes much of this recent book to what he calls the "crisis of purpose and vocation now raging in the profession" (135).

In an essay entitled, "Theory, Pragmatism, and Politics," West explores the "vocation of the humanistic intellectual," an issue that he says is a "political and ideological one," even though, as in each of the writers we have just examined, this issue "surfaces in our time as a discourse about professionalism" (94). Although West acknowledges that the term "vocation" is certainly out of favor these days, in pragmatic terms that Berthoff would characterize as thinking about thinking, West argues that the late twentieth century is precisely the historical moment at which teachers must "rethink, revise, and retain a notion of vocation":

> [W]e live at a particular historical moment in which a serious interrogation regarding "vocations" of intellectuals and academicians in American society can *contribute to a more enabling and empowering sense of the moral and political dimensions of our functioning in the present-day academy.* To take seriously one's vocation as an intellectual is to justify in moral and political terms why one pursues a rather privileged life of the mind in a world that seems to require forms of more direct and urgent action. (94)

West sees an intimate and necessary connection between intellect and action, between theory and practice, and he broadens the definition of practice to extend beyond the classroom. West comments in this passage on precisely what Will calls the "comfortable professoriate," and he admits the privilege of an academic life. He goes on, though, to insist that if this life is taken seriously, examined carefully, then it must also include the necessity of considering seriously what action such a life requires. For West, as all his work on race in North America so clearly shows, that action extends beyond the classroom, but we hear him speaking of the practice of teaching as the consequence, in action, of the privileged life of the mind and books. The life of the mind must be a life of moral and political action; in action lie the consequences of scholarship, research, theory, writing, and reading. In order to justify, explain, and live with our "careers," then, teachers need to pull together the life of the mind and its consequences; in other words, for teaching to be possible, we have to consider how theory about knowledge fits with the ways in which we put that knowledge to use with students. To go further, a teacher must help students see the connection as well, looking and looking again at how what's being taught and learned can be used beyond the course itself.

Looking and looking again, examining your suppositions, theorizing about practice, and practicing your theory are activities that too often seem unusual or out of place in schools and universities, for both teachers and students. Berthoff lays much of the blame on the prevalence of "dyadic" conceptions of language, where "meaning" and "knowledge" are regarded as originating from either within or without, with arguments abounding about these sites of origin (1991, 280). Berthoff says that the either/or dualism of most thinking about language, writing, and reading leads to empty pedagogies of exhortation or despair, with very little connection to the writer, the reader, or the world in which the text is read/written. When she asks if teaching is still possible, she calls for a kind of reflective teaching and theorizing, where both teaching and theory are mediated in a triadic rather than dyadic system. Just as the relationship between word and meaning is mediated by the referent that puts the two together, so theory and practice are mediated by the kinds of reflection that allow each to be influenced by the other.

Peter Elbow has encouraged the profession for decades now to embrace this kind of "mediated" view, to play both the "doubting and believing games," but institutional and professional pressure make the tension difficult to maintain. Increasingly, despite the shorthand use of the terms "theory/practice" as one term, theory seems reserved for seminars and scholarly journals, while practice is relegated to "mere" experience, unconnected to theory. Those who would name themselves primarily as teachers seem increasingly hostile to theory, increasingly frustrated by attempts, their own or outsiders, to make it govern or explain their practice. Practice is sometimes seen as the only worthwhile enterprise, and theory becomes almost a pejorative in some contexts. "I didn't come here to talk theory," a presenter at NCTE says, and this remark is greeted with applause. And those who consider themselves primarily theorists too often fail to consider the consequences of theory in their own classrooms, and for the teachers they are "training" in critical theory.

Two of the most influential forces in composition teaching today—the workshop approach, as presented by teachers like Nancie Atwell, and the ascendancy of critical postmodern theory—seem at times to represent two different disciplinary communities, two ways of seeing the "action" required of teachers of writing. Practitioners, left only with "lore," focus on examining classroom experience, studying students' experience, and generalizing from there about overall methods; theorists, enthralled mostly in texts and models, focus on examining relationships out of context, sometimes without looking at all to their own or their students' experience. Many theorists, scholars, and teachers, of course, insist on the necessary relationship between experience and theory, and many work hard to examine and enact that relationship, but increasingly, it seems, the structures of the discipline, its hierarchical obsessions, its drive for status, and its insistence on labels keep teachers separated from theory, and theorists unconnected to the lived experience of those they are teaching. In English departments there is a sad irony in the way that story and theory come to occupy different, opposing positions.

Well-known teachers like Lucy Calkins and Nancie Atwell sometimes seem to advocate the position that the only way people *can* learn is through story, or experience, and yet teachers, especially student-teachers, are often frustrated by their attempts to make someone else's experience connect to their own. Nancie Atwell's popular book *In the Middle: Writing, Reading, and Learning with Adolescents* begins with the words "I confess," and continues as a conversion story, using the metaphor of "coming out from behind the big desk" to design a student-centered curriculum, complete with student choice about reading, writing, time, energy. Atwell's enthusiasm and belief in her newly-designed reading and writing workshops are contagious; her "results" are convincing, to say the least. The entire book is inspirational, if a bit daunting, to new or would-be teachers. We have watched students react, first, with hope to Atwell's careful accounts of her students' progress in writing, and then seen them react with cynicism and doubt about their own prospects of creating such a classroom: "That might be fine for her; but I'm going to be teaching in the real world." "Where are her 'regular' students?" "How can she get away with that? My principal would never let me do that." Thus, what is intended as a book to help teachers believe in possibilities for changed classrooms very often ends up being dismissed as fantasy, an unrealistic, concocted story intended to make Atwell seem otherworldly.

Perhaps it's just not enough to tell one's own story, however compelling the story might be. Without the theoretical background and thinking that informs the changes they document, and without overt discussions of how they managed to effect such change, Atwell's and Calkins's classrooms can seem utopian, unconnected to the real contexts in which their readers work, and we have found our students reacting too often with cynicism or hopelessness to these teachers' testimonials, instead of being inspired to make changes in their own contexts. The implications of untheorized teachers' stories are that stories are all teachers need, and that the kind of support, abstraction, justification that theory provides is not useful or necessary. And to call stories about teaching "theory" about teaching is to conflate two terms that need to be examined in relationship. Central to both Calkins's and Atwell's stories of their transformation as teachers is the kind of reflection that would bring theory and practice together. But, perhaps in an attempt to "tone it down," the theoretical, philosophical beliefs that guide these teachers' practices and changes are oddly missing from their reports.

Teaching stories like Atwell's and Calkins's can be dismissed as "mere" practice or celebrated as useful practical knowledge: Some teachers are hostile to theory, because they do not see the connection to their lived experiences in the classroom or their reading of the literature they love. Yet the opposite perspective leads to an equally disturbing trend: Other teachers embrace theory wholeheartedly *in theory*, but do not use theory to reflect on or change their own classrooms or implications for re-reading literature. If reflective theory-making is missing from teaching stories like Atwell's and Calkins's, then reflections about practice are absent from much of current critical theory. This opposite perspective from elevating practice as the only method for making knowledge yields another prevalent and disturbing trend: the study of "pure" critical theory—postmodern, feminist, post-process—out of context, as an "out-of-body" experience, existing for its own sake, disembodied from living texts and lived experience. The "postmodern condition" described by any number of theorists from François Lyotard to Richard Rorty has made the divorce between reflecting and doing appear final. When Stanley Fish writes in *Doing What Comes Naturally* that "I have nothing to sell except the not very helpful news that practice has nothing to do with theory" (1989, 365), he does more than shrug his shoulders at theory's uses in practical pedagogical contexts. As a theorist himself, with a book that explores and explains what theory, and not practice, does in knowledge making, he diminishes and displaces practice to a realm that speculation, judgment, and philosophy can't reach and supposedly wouldn't want to. The tone of Fish's statement strikes the reader's ear as vaguely—if gaily—hopeless. Its message is undeniably cynical, and cynicism is increasingly popular, at least in theory.

Fish arrives at his conclusion about the irrelevance of theory for practice through a long and fascinating analysis of the implications of anti-foundationalism, along the way exploring what he calls "theory-hope" and "theory-fear." Fish goes to a lot of trouble to explain why current critical theory cannot speak to changes in practices, or even to method itself. Adopting a thoroughly anti-foundational stance, and embracing the concept that every act, thought, stance is steeped in historical, cultural situatedness lead many to hope for wholesale change, change that comes from unclouded vision, from newly seeing the situated sources of old (and current) views. But, Fish argues, that kind of "theory-hope" refuses to see the way current critical theory, by its very definition, clouds vision as well: "Neither can anti-foundationalism have the consequences for which some of its proponents *hope*, the consequences of freeing us from the hold of unwarranted absolutes so that we may more flexibly pursue the goals of human flourishing or liberal conversation" (324). Fish explains that anti-foundationalism, "the *going* argument," leads its advocates to hope that since they now realize that their beliefs about truth and experience are not a priori, not "imposed upon us by the world, or imprinted in our brains," but are constituted from "the practices of ideologically motivated communities," that they can cast those beliefs aside and choose freely, instead, convictions that more closely mirror the ideal context they desire. Fish argues, however, that this "going theory" has little to say about consequences, or the possibilities for action:

> Anti-foundationalist fear and anti-foundationalist hope turn out to differ only in emphasis. . . . Both make the mistake of thinking that anti-foundationalism, by demonstrating the contextual source of conviction, cuts the ground out from under conviction—it is just that, for one party, this is good news and, for the other, it is the news that chaos has come again. But in fact, anti-foundationalism says nothing about what we can now do or not do; it is an account of what we have always been doing and what we cannot help but do. . . . (325)

For teachers, who often fall victim to what Fish calls "theory-fear," and what Tom Byers has named "pomophobia," the threat of theory is its chaotic disconnection from experience, its inability to explain practice or suggest methods for change. Fish says: "As a searching critique of method, anti-foundationalism cannot itself be made the basis of a method without losing its anti-foundationalist character" (351). For theorists, who persist in what Fish calls "theory-hope," the promise of theory is the implied connection to experience, the "narrative in which conversion to a theory leads directly to a revolution in practice" (354). But, Fish insists, this conversion story demands a foundationalist hero, someone who has discovered "truth" and now "returns to implement it." Once converted to theory, however, Fish admits that "this is a hard move to make or not make because it brings so little immediate satisfaction and leaves the would-be theorist with so little to do" (355). He concludes with the "small" news that "not only does being converted to anti-foundationalism bring with it no pedagogical payoff; being opposed to anti-foundationalism entails no pedagogical penalty" (353).

Fish's sense of futility and stalemate pervades much of the academic conversation about the postmodern era, even when that sense remains unexamined. Linda Hutcheon's *A Poetics of Postmodernism* generalizes about underpinnings of postmodern criticism, what she calls its "poetics": "There is no dialectic in the postmodern: the self-reflexive remains distinct from its traditionally-accepted contrary—the historiopolitical context in which it is embedded" (1988, x). There is no dialectic because there is no real consensus possible, no site from which to examine positions or practices. Postmodernism raises questions, Hutcheon notes, "but it never offers answers that are anything but provisional and contextually determined (and limited)" (xi). Hutcheon offers in her assessment an apologetic of sorts for postmodern thought and its consequences; anti-foundationalism has allowed thinkers to get beyond a false notion of objectivity and universality of experience in all kinds of arenas, including the reading and writing of texts. But in its insistence on anti-totalitarianism, it refuses all generalities, except for the not very helpful one that there is no generality. It thus evades responsibility for its own premises by suggesting that words, or ideas, are separable from actions.

Much of postmodern theory is based on such dyadic conceptions of knowledge, relying on a binary, either/or view of the objects of transformation (high and low culture, literature vs. text, for example), which necessitates the breaking down of the privilege that accrues to one side of the pair and an elevating of the other side. In empowering the suppressed parts of the system, the binaries remain, however, and the consequences remain unexamined. John McGowan, while accepting postmodernism's epistemological attack on foundational principles, argues that there is still much transformative work to do: "Too much postmodern thought chooses to continue its anarchistic demonstrations against the existing order, demonstrations that appear intended more to prove the agent's independence and purity than to address seriously the transformation of that order or the agent's own involvement in and/or complicity within it" (1991, 16).

The explosion of postmodern, postfeminist, postprocess theories has been aimed at challenging the Western philosophical tradition, and such challenges to patriarchy and privilege ought to give hope to scholars and teachers, but the Western tradition has not been fundamentally altered with these new theories, and that paradox can lead to despair or cynicism. In fact, those who write critical theory are writing within an institutional system of scholarship and research that operates with thoroughly traditional forms of power. The most powerful postmodern theorists can easily be read as the Richards and Warren of our own critical day, and none of their debates have been won or lost, much less changed the way teachers conduct the business of teaching. McGowan describes the difficulty in actually outlining what a "practical politics of heterogeneity" would look like: because of postmodernism's distrust of generalizations, of "wholes," any suggestions for outcomes "rarely move beyond vague recommendations that generally appear hopeless the moment one begins seriously to flesh them out" (21). In fact, one of the real ironies of current critical theory is its elevation to the level of "truth" the insistence that there is no truth to be found. And although the ideal of a completely pluralistic order informs most recent theoretical work, Stanley Aronowitz admits that the ideal of "radical democracy" exists only as an "ethical *a priori.*" (1987, 104). Jean Franco goes so far as to describe postmodernism as "a withdrawal from human action" (104).

Kurt Spellmeyer's article, "After Theory: From Textuality to Attunement with the World," is a strong and clear-headed description of this disjunction between theory and action and its inevitable consequence:

> Theory, in other words, has outlived its own "death," but its survival gives cold comfort to all the former converts who have irretrievably lost their faith. For those of us no longer charmed by the magic, by the myth, of the pursuit of signs—what other path remains if we want to be more than perpetually "post-"? (894)

If, as Spellmeyer implies, current theoretical positions cannot situate democracy or freedom or change in external principles, and at the same time remain always suspicious and cynical about human agents of change because they are constructed by the powerful contexts around them, then what, indeed, is left for a teacher to do? In this climate, where neither stories nor theories serve the end of reflective teaching, teachers can easily become cynical, seeing themselves as cogs in a machine they cannot control, or as co-conspirators fighting an oppressive regime or, most likely, as pawns controlled by that regime. Whatever independence teachers like Atwell and Calkins might achieve is seen as a fluke, something out of a romance; whatever independence teachers may achieve themselves is won by inches and celebrated in solitary silence: "I just close my door and teach." If it's all the same no matter what, or if it's always unique and predetermined no matter what, then why bother? And if the system is always already corrupt, and a teacher's actions are always determined by the context of that system, then why bother? Teaching not only does not seem possible; it begins to seem positively irrelevant.

Spellmeyer describes himself as "demoralized" by what he calls a "uniquely unpleasant event"—a meeting of the New Jersey Basic Skills Council, charged with assessing the public schools:

> Fourteen years and many millions of dollars into a campaign of twelfth-grade exit testing, the Council had assembled the data to "prove" that thousands of graduates from the poorest urban neighborhoods—in Camden, Newark, and Jersey City—were functionally illiterate. But the data themselves were *all* we had; none of us knew why the scores were so low, and no one could explain with much clarity—although we were ostensibly the best in our field— how we should respond. (1996, 895)

The ensuing silence leads Spellmeyer to reflect on the ways in which this elite group could so easily apply the label of illiteracy and devise methods to measure its spread "without ever knowing what the word really meant." In other words, they could not name literacy/illiteracy by examining either its origins or its consequences in context. He despairs, too, of the group's solution to the problem they could label but not name: to begin instruction "at the zero point, proceeding as if these 'children' had 'no language' of their own" (895), knowing that this solution would not work now, just as it had not worked before. This realization, that neither theory nor practice makes a difference, leads Spellmeyer to propose an alternative rooted in both the past and the future:

> What we need is nothing less than a paradigm shift: turning from the threadbare ideology of "the text," we might start to explore an alternative so mundane that we have passed it over time after time in our scramble for sophistication and prestige. That alternative is ordinary sensuous life, which is not an "effect" of how we think but the ground of thought itself, or so I want to argue here. At this late hour, when theory's successors can teach us nothing really new, what prevents us from returning to "the arts" by a long-forgotten path— the arts imagined as traditions of experience that intensify our sense of living in and with the world? (894)

Neither "mere" practicality nor "mere" theorizing, then, will serve teachers who know that thought and life must be related in the work they do in and out of the classroom. One of the central beliefs upon which this book rests is West's "prophetic pragmatism," which, like

Spellemyer's paradigm shift, provides a counterpoint to postmodern theory and postmodern practicality. West embraces pragmatic philosophy because "pragmatism has emerged within contemporary literary criticism in relation to two fundamental issues: the role of theory and the vocation of the humanistic intellectual" (1993a, 90). Connecting the words theory and vocation deliberately, West calls upon intellectuals (teachers, scholars, critics, researchers, professionals) to act and believe in their role as "critical organic catalysts," grounded both inside and outside the academy: "To be an engaged progressive intellectual is to be a critical organic catalyst whose vocation is to fuse the best of the life of the mind from within the academy with the best of the organized forces for greater democracy and freedom from outside the academy" (103). West's pragmatic stance is more charitable toward "grand theory" than those trapped in theory-fear and more skeptical of grand theory than those lured by theory-hope. At every level, West's prophetic pragmatism is tied to practice, to questions of what it means to claim the vocation of a teacher.

We name West's stance *romantic/pragmatic rhetoric* although this is our term, not his. We will move farther back in history than West does in his explication of pragmatism to look for the sources of pragmatism in American romanticism and its predecessors, and we will move further out than West does into the classroom as a site for the romantic/pragmatic intellectual's work. We want, of course, for this book to answer "yes" to Bethoff's question "Is teaching still possible?" and to define the vocation of teaching in ways that inextricably combine theory and practice. We want to provide an answer that casts teaching as something other than what theorists can't speak to and theory as something other than what teachers cannot use. We want, to put it simply, to work out a theoretical stance that will provide a reason to believe in the vocation of a teacher as intellectual and as social agent of change.

Obviously, the title of this book reveals our own bias in favor of belief, most importantly the belief that change is possible. That might seem "romantic"; belief in possibilities, the future, or in agents of change is often called "romantic." When the word is applied that way, it's often used in opposition to the word "pragmatic": what's "realistic," "practical," "normal," or "possible." At the same time, the practical, the realistic, and the possible are dismissed as well, as only "pragmatic," opposed to what's deeply considered or visionary. Both words—

romantic and *pragmatic*—are used most often as pejorative terms for outdated or theoretically empty positions. Teachers who think that the worst of their students can succeed; rhetoricians who believe that writers wield power; and theorists who attend to the imagination are all labeled "romantics." Teachers who begin with where students are; rhetoricians who focus on audience; and theorists who point to real contexts are all labeled as "pragmatic." In the following pages, we show how much these stereotypical labels distort historical reality and limit current practice.

Paulo Freire is a teacher we name as a *romantic/pragmatic rhetorician,* and he begins *A Pedagogy of Hope* by rescuing romanticism from its stereotype even as he opposes that new definition to the stereotype of the practical: "We are surrounded by a pragmatic discourse that would have us adapt to the facts of reality. *Dream,* and *utopia,* are called not only useless, but positively impeding" (1994, 7). Freire insists that dream and utopia are not useless concepts but real visions, particularly necessary in the face of what he sees as the pervasiveness of empirical, fatalistic, positivistic approaches to problems, which he equates with "pragmatic" thinking. The book is devoted to rekindling hope in the possibility of change in the culture and the systems in which teachers work. "I do not understand human existence, and the struggle needed to improve it, apart from hope and dream. Hope is an ontological need. Hopelessness is but hope that has lost its bearings and become a distortion of that ontological need" (8). While Freire celebrates the virtues of "romantic" thinking, of the possibilities of hope and dream, he answers his critics who have accused him of falling into the traps of stereotypical romanticism—of being too idealistic, too ideological, too individualistic, too hopeful. The kind of romantic thinking Freire uses is far from the stereotype of "unrealistic" and "dreamy": "The idea that hope alone will transform the world, and action undertaken in that kind of naïveté, is an excellent route to hopelessness, pessimism, and fatalism" (8). Hope is rigorous, intellectual. It requires, in Freire's words, struggle and action. Freire believes that the romantic is in danger of being overtaken by the pragmatic, and that's why he emphasizes hope over doubt. Although Freire opposes the concept of hope to the stereotypically pragmatic, his insistence on consequence and on action is truly pragmatic: "The essential thing . . . is this: hope as an ontological need demands an anchoring in practice. . . . That is why there's no hope in sheer hopefulness" (9).

Freire's life's work embodies romantic/pragmatic stances; Freire's work is a struggle to put the concept of belief together with action, to insist that ideas have consequences. His word *conscientizao* means consciousness enACTed. With this term, he counters the tendency to think dyadically, which always leads to one side of the pair being privileged over the other, as Berthoff warns. This tendency to think in opposition is so strong that Freire himself falls into it when he calls the pragmatic the enemy of hopeful. Yet one of the central concepts of pragmatism is mediation, the premise that ideas can move beyond their unique or opposing characteristics and toward relationship. Pragmatism itself offers a method of moving beyond dualism, recognizing that a third principle can lead thinkers out of the traps of ideological narrowness, meaningless debate, and fatalism. *Pragmatic* and *pragmatism* are not simple terms, and neither are *romantic* or *romanticism*, even though these are names people believe they know how to use. Romanticism and pragmatism both operate from principles of mediation, and we argue that romanticism and pragmatism together offer ways of thinking again about the debates that continue in composition and English studies.

To rescue both terms—romantic and pragmatic—from their traditional labels and limiting connotations, we will rename them together, in order to look again at their histories and their current incarnations in theory and practice, both of which are currently obscured because romanticism has been studied and categorized so much and pragmatism hardly at all. These two names describe and argue for a set of principles and actions, and renaming them together allows them to become something other than labels; they become generative words, words to think with. We will investigate romantic and pragmatic philosophy, in historical as well as ideological ways, but it won't be our aim to separate the two, because they are intertwined historically, philosophically, and practically. Pragmatism in fact offers a method of explaining how principles of romanticism can operate in the world. A "romantic/pragmatic rhetoric" of teaching would recast traditional assumptions and definitions about the role of belief in teaching and in research, about process and progress, and about what is theoretical and what is practical. It would have teachers look and look again at their histories, assumptions, and behaviors, understanding what looking entails, and what naming implies.

As teachers and researchers in university settings, we daily face the difficulty of mediating between the practical and the theoretical.

Most teachers are continually pulled one way and then another. The pull of theory is seductive, given the desire to escape the messiness of individual difference and the fear of mere subjectivity. The pull of practice is just as seductive, given the temptation to close the door on what seems out of individual control and just to concentrate on the local instance. Even more difficult is the need to remain restless and unsettled in our work. To continue to mediate requires, as Freire says, continual "watchfulness," continual willingness to welcome change. Because teachers find it so difficult to keep thinking at once theoretically and practically, globally and locally, our students face the same troublesome difficulties. Graduate students tend to embrace theory or cling to practice, but their work in courses seldom helps them find the strands that would pull together their scholarly and teacherly lives, or to explore the implications of the theories they learn to invest in so strongly. And for younger students, theory and its implications for their own practices are rarely if ever mentioned. Students learn to be expedient when it comes to course requirements, final grades, and schedules.

It's not enough to tell people that theory and practice go together. There must be more than labeling or pairing of terms; there must be a method of demonstrating how reflection and action interact and a renaming that enables that the pairing of theory and practice, action and reflection, to result in positive change. bell hooks, another romantic/pragmatic teacher, renames her own practice this way. She explains in *Teaching to Transgress* that she "came to theory because [she] was hurting" (1994, 61). In an institutional context of compartmentalization, racism, and patriarchy, she found a "sanctuary in theorizing, in making sense out of what was happening, a place where I could imagine possible futures, a place where life could be lived differently. . . . Fundamentally, I learned from this experience that theory could be a healing place" (61). Like Freire, though, hooks does not stop with simple hope about what theory might do. She warns that "theory is not inherently healing, liberatory, or revolutionary. It fulfills this function only when we ask that it do so and direct our theorizing toward this end" (61). This questioning of theory through experience and action is a romantic/pragmatic stance, just as close observation of practice and its consequences theoretically is a romantic/pragmatic method.

Cornel West, Paulo Freire, and bell hooks are not directly involved in composition or English studies. But, put next to Miller, Tompkins, and North, and Will, we believe they offer a vision of the vocation of the teacher that resists cynicism, elitism, expediency, and despair. A closer look at these teachers, in the context of a larger look at romanticism and pragmatism, will, we hope, yield the kind of inquiry that happens when faith is tested with doubt, when theory is challenged by action. These romantic/pragmatic rhetoricians are teachers and theorists who connect private vision with public action, understand the possibilities and limits of community, and create systematic methods for testing beliefs.

Romantic/pragmatic rhetoric is not a new phenomenon, as we will show. This philosophy and method has been around, available to those who share the vocation of teaching, for a long time. Like most theories, it has taken some twists and turns, fallen in and out of favor, and, in the latest renaissance in composition studies, been largely ignored. We will trace the path that romanticism and pragmatism followed, looking historically at their beginnings in North America and their influences and incarnations in the history of writing instruction. We look back, not simply to give an historical accounting, but to demonstrate the living quality and timely relevance of romantic/pragmatic rhetoric. West's work reminds teachers of the power and use of pragmatism; we will examine the romanticism inherent in pragmatism. Freire and hooks show teachers the necessity of belief and faith; we will show that inherently pragmatic stance within romanticism. We believe that a new look at romanticism, despite its dismissal in the current climate of doubt, and a new look at pragmatism, despite its diminished status in the latest context of theory, might be in order in composition right now. Such a study, we hope, might provide a reason to believe in the vocation of teaching and its uses in the world. In the following pages, we will locate methods for what Freire names as "educating our hope."

TWO

THE DOCTRINE OF USE
Seeds of Romantic/Pragmatic Rhetoric

> [The tragicomic vision] encourages me to put a premium
> on garnering resources from a vanishing past in a deca-
> dent present in order to keep alive a tempered hope for
> the future, a hope against hope that human empathy and
> compassion may survive against the onslaught of human
> barbarity, brutality, and bestiality.
>
> —Cornel West, *Keeping Faith*

> This use of the world includes the preceding uses, as parts
> of itself.
>
> —Ralph Waldo Emerson, *Nature*

At the end of his introduction to *Possible Lives: The Promise of Public
Education in America,* Mike Rose invokes an American romantic poet to
illustrate his purpose for traveling across the United States to visit,
study, and write about American public schools: "'I refer,' wrote Walt
Whitman, 'to a Democracy that is yet unborn'" (1995, 10). It is no
accident that Whitman appears in this opening, or that Dewey's *Experience and Education* is cited prominently in the acknowledgments to this
book. In fact, Rose's whole project in this massive description of public education in the 1990s can be read as an enactment of both the
romantic philosophy of the public poetry of Whitman and the romantic pragmatism of the educator of the people, John Dewey. Certainly
Rose means to "educate the hope," as Freire says, of teachers, students, parents, professors, and the public. Rose states his purpose in
writing—to "help us think in a different way" (4)—so that the "dismissive, despairing" discussion about education in this country, which
Rose says is "shutting down the civic imagination" (1), might be turned
into "the kind of talk that comes from thoughtful work and leads to
thoughtful action" (10).

The connection of thought to action here is obviously rhetorical, since rhetoric requires hearers to act, and it is also pragmatic, since pragmatism requires inquirers to investigate consequences. But Rose's rhetoric in *Possible Lives* is also romantic, romantic in his insistence on paying attention to the "social, moral, and aesthetic dimensions of teaching and learning" (2), and romantic in his call for a new kind of language about teaching that might replace what he calls the current "rhetoric of decline" (2) and "loss of faith" (5). While visiting public school classrooms around the country for four years, observing and collaborating with teachers, students, parents, and administrators, Rose found islands of hope in a national context where "public education itself is threatened by cynicism and retreat, by the cold rapture of the market, by thin measure and the loss of civic imagination" (433). In stories told with anger, elation, and despair, Rose calls for a different kind of public critique of schools, one that "opens discursive space for inspired teaching, for courage, for achievement against odds, for successful struggle" (4). In other words, he is calling for a dialectic between reality and possibility, and his book offers to readers the "rich detailed images of possibility" that Rose says the public discussion of education so desperately needs (4).

Rose does not use the words "romantic" or "pragmatic" to describe his stance, but in evoking both Whitman and Dewey and in his own language of hope and possibility, Rose is carrying on a long American tradition of rhetoric that *Reason to Believe* seeks to explore, explain, and revive. Romantic/pragmatic rhetoric as a philosophical position may not have been named or claimed by its practitioners (or its detractors), but it's a mode of action and thought that teachers, philosophers, and scholars have nonetheless embraced throughout recent history. It's seen most clearly in the work of those thinkers who overtly explore the dialectic between what seem diametrically opposed doctrines of belief and doubt. We've mentioned a few of the practitioners already; the rest of this book will investigate writers, civil servants, preachers, and teachers whose work consciously or unaware exhibits those qualities we're defining as inherent in romantic/pragmatic rhetoric. The practitioners we discuss first are some of the earliest American romantics and pragmatists, some of them writing and teaching long before Romanticism became a term set out by Wordsworth in the Preface to the *Lyrical Ballads* or pragmatism became an American philosophy popularized by William James. We want to show how romanticism and pragmatism together construct a rhetoric uniquely suited, as Whitman says, to "creating America," and, as Rose argues, to sustaining the democratic experiment of education.

To see romantic/pragmatic rhetoric as one concept requires a bit of a leap of faith, especially given the common (and current) assumptions associated with each part of this new term. Traditional definitions of "romantic" and "rhetorical" appear as oppositions, perhaps capable of being juxtaposed but not in any way connected. The stereotypical primary tenet of romanticism—the search for and glorification of self—seems profoundly antirhetorical, or at least a-rhetorical, just as the purview of rhetoric—persuasion of another person or a group toward a desired end—seems antiromantic. And the popular conception of pragmatism, which casts it as a "commonsense," thus a-theoretical, stance, places pragmatism in opposition to theories of both romanticism and rhetoric. Our project is to collapse and elide all three terms into one, and we argue that historically the three have operated together as an important but neglected strand of American philosophy. Historically, however, in education, and even until recently in philosophy, pragmatism has been ignored; it's the opposition between "romanticism" and "rhetoric" that we most want to collapse first. Looking at two of the most famous characterizations of "romantic" and "rhetorical" language illustrates the division:

> Eloquence is heard, poetry is overheard. . . . All poetry is in the nature of soliloquy. . . . Poetry is feeling confessing itself to itself, in moments of solitude. (Mill 1967)

> Rhetoric is the faculty of observing in any given case the available means of persuasion. (Aristotle 1954)

Mill's definition of poetry does in fact deny the rhetorical. When the individual and feelings are the proper object of study, the primary site of discovery, and the only possible object of both, an audience becomes almost, if not quite, beside the point. The famous line about lyric poetry as "overheard" by a reader is the culmination of the a-rhetorical definition of romanticism. In Mill's formulation, the reader is an eavesdropper in the real conversation, the one among poet, soul, and nature. There can be, then, no rhetorical triangle of speaker, subject, and audience; instead, there's a line, from speaker to subject and back again, with the reader a small, unconnected point outside the line's boundary. If communication or persuasion occurs, it happens by accident more than by design. The emphasis on expression as the rationale for composing underlies what is labeled romantic theory, and that label leads to the vision of romantic writers waiting for intuition, demanding isolation, and embodying uniqueness.

No less does the stereotypical definition of rhetoric seem to put it in direct opposition to romantic values. When the subject for study becomes the means toward desired ends in discourse, as in Aristotle's definition of rhetoric, the emphasis on self seems wrongheaded, as many of the current debates about the expressive purposes of composition courses illustrate. In rhetoric, it's the given case or context in combination with the immediate audience that constitutes value in expression. There is no overhearing of discourse going on in rhetoric; the message is forthcoming and—the writer hopes—irresistible. The attention in traditional rhetoric has been on the constructed hearer or reader, and on a self created to most effectively persuade that reader. And in much twentieth-century popular, if not academic, thinking about rhetoric, there is more than a tinge of cynicism in the way rhetoric is labeled as manipulative, deceitful, concerned only with effect, not origin.

These stereotypes about rhetoric also inform popular conceptions of what it means to be pragmatic. Stereotypically, the pragmatist looks for the most efficient means to an end, without stopping to question much since stopping would reduce efficiency and practicality. A pragmatist is conceived of as neutral, not focused on self or audience, but, like the stereotypical rhetorician, constructed for the expedient purpose of delivering and completing a message. All three terms are used popularly in both positive and negative ways, but most often they are used as dismissive labels, as *merely* romantic, *simply* pragmatic, or *just* rhetoric.

English courses in college and high school continue to define these terms in such stereotypical ways. When students think of romanticism, they think of foggy moors and declarations of eternal love; when they think of rhetoric, they think of sleazy politicians and television commercials. Neither teachers nor students think much about pragmatism at all, except in its most colloquial sense as a kind of useful behavior for meeting requirements or deadlines. As a philosophical system unique to the United States, it has been, until recently, largely ignored in the twentieth century; one result of this omission is that, without pragmatism's mediating function, romanticism and rhetoric have remained conceptual and practical opposites.

The stereotypical and dichotomous characterizations about what's romantic and what's rhetorical might seem exaggerated until one looks at the work of writers of composition who fall into easy generalizations and categorizations about the kinds and uses of language that writing courses should be teaching. In fact, the opposition of romantic and rhetorical stances has dominated much of the scholarly conversation in composition and rhetoric for the last twenty-five years. Ever since James Kinneavy's 1971 *A Theory of Discourse*, there has been, in theory if not in practice, an unwavering line drawn between "expressive discourse" and discourse that "persuades" or "refers/informs." Kinneavy, of course, drew on M. H. Abrams's 1953 study of romanticism, which divided the work of art, and criticism in general, into elements of the work itself (objective theories), the artist (expressive theories), the universe (mimetic theories), and the audience (pragmatic theories) (6–7). While Abrams was primarily interested in classifying the aims of literary criticism, Kinneavy sought to explain the relationship of thought to expression and to identify four basic aims in discourse, depending on the rhetorical emphasis: expressive (writer), referential (subject), persuasive (audience), and literary (text). Kinneavy did not see these categories as fixed or mutually exclusive; in fact, he continually emphasized that these aims overlap in almost any discourse, and he was careful to warn that they do not constitute a hierarchy.

But almost from the publication of this landmark book, composition has read these aims as hierarchical; at the very least, they have been analyzed as polar opposites, for a variety of rhetorical reasons. One could, we suppose, blame Aristotle for Kinneavy's scheme, since his rhetorical triangle formed the basis of Kinneavy's classification. But researchers who investigated actual writers, rather than texts, also divided language according to an emphasis on self or other. In the same year that Kinneavy published his *Theory of Discourse,* Janet Emig's classification of students' writing into "reflexive" and "extensive" modes paved the way for a generation of work in composition that opposed writers to information, writers to audiences, self to school, self to society. Linda Flower's arguments about "writer-" and "reader-based" prose followed this same division, although Flower privileged writing that focused on a reader, while Emig was arguing that "reflexive" writing needed more attention in school. The "process" movement of the 1970s seemed to focus on the individual writer, but "the writing process" itself always moved outward to an audience. Add the psycholinguistic influences on composition in the late 1980s, which led theorists to argue that "inner" speech needed more emphasis or that "social" speech should be the goal of writing teachers, and the stage was set for an interpretive paradigm in composition that, for twenty years, has centered around self/other divisions, divisions that quickly arrange themselves into hierarchies.

One of the most influential and long-standing hierarchies in the field has been James Berlin's division of the field into "expressive, cognitive, and social-epistemic" foundations for theory and practice in teaching writing. These "competing theories" were first described in 1986 by Lester Faigley, who presented them in a sort of historical progression and who argued that only a "synthesis" of the three, based in historical awareness, would lead composition to the disciplinary status it longed for only ten years ago (1986, 539). But James Berlin's work set these categories in opposition, not synthesis. In both "Rhetoric and Ideology" and *Rhetoric and Reality*, Berlin, like Faigley, presents expressive, cognitive, and social rhetoric in historical progression, and composition growing ever more disciplinary as it moved from self to society, from simple to complex, from ideologically naive to ideologically complex and aware. Berlin acknowledges that "ideology is always pluralistic; a given historical moment displaying a variety of competing ideologies and a given individual reflecting one or another permutation of these conflicts" (1988, 479). However, Berlin clearly opposes these three "rhetorics." Cognitive rhetoric, he says "refuses the ideological question altogether, claiming the neutrality of science" (478); in other words, it is merely practical. Expressionist rhetoric seeks to locate the "individual's authentic nature," often in ideological resistance to existing systems, but its isolationism makes it easily co-opted by the forces it resists (487). In other words, it is romantically naive. Berlin finally argues that only social-epistemic rhetoric, which "attempts to place the question of ideology at the center of teaching writing," can lead to socially responsible writing pedagogy (492). Berlin suggests a clear choice between social-epistemic rhetoric as an "overtly historicized alternative" and the other, less sophisticated rhetorics. This three-part taxonomy, useful for a field in the process of defining itself, has become canonical in composition studies over the last ten years;

and the story of composition's growth is now told in terms of the "social turn" the discipline took after Berlin's overview pointed the way.

In all these attempts to define composition, the specter of romanticism has always hovered, sometimes portrayed as a seductive yet dangerous presence to be beaten back, subdued, or overcome, sometimes described as a "garret" that writers wish they could retreat to, and sometimes cast as an infantile stage to be passed through and dismissed once writers achieve a mature, rigorous rhetorical sense of context and purpose (see Brodkey 1987a). Two particular examples will illustrate this overreaction to the romantic presence in composition and rhetoric. In an article for *Rhetoric Review*, David Russell characterizes the "neo-Romantic expressivists" like Peter Elbow and Ken Macrorie as those who value the character of the "old romanticism: the inner promptings, originality, imagination, integrity, authentic voice" (1988, 143). The problem is, as Russell explains it, that these romantic principles lie outside *rhetorical* principles and are thus subject to attack: "If writing is seen as essentially subjective, a mysterious response to experience, and its teaching a set of techniques evolving from that response, then composition courses can and will be attacked as an 'intellectual vacuum'" (144).

Russell repeatedly equates romantic with antisociety as well as antitheoretical or at least a-intellectual. Romantic views, he notes, have been consistently challenged by other views "which see writing within a social context that transcends the individual" (145). Russell attacks the romantics as elite, a product of "liberal culture" at the beginning of the twentieth century. Berlin, too, locates the sources of "expressionist" approaches in the "liberal culture" movements at the turn of the century: "This rhetoric was elitist and aristocratic, contending that the aim of writing instruction in the English department ought to be to encourage those few students who possess genius. For the rest, courses in literature should provide lessons in taste. . ." (1987, 35). Seeing writing classes as sites of social critique and democratic education, both Russell and Berlin find "romantic" approaches antiquated. Bound in a literary tradition that emphasized individual genius, romanticism's model of communication, they argue, does not work in a contemporary writing classroom. Rhetoric, with its emphasis on the communicative context and the sharing of knowledge, is a better model, especially for a field seeking disciplinary status separate from literary studies. But in their attempt to privilege rhetoric, they are forced by their own arguments to diminish the rhetorical character of romanticism. Sherrie Gradin's book *Romancing Rhetorics* tries to connect contemporary social expressivism with romanticism through an examination of each theory's rhetorical tradition. She explains the disciplinary reasons for this opposition:

> Critics of expressivism are involved in a power struggle within their own discipline and within the larger field of English Studies. As compositionists, we have had to fight and argue our way into disciplinary status. This hunger for power and authority within English Studies leads to the desire to create hierarchy and to establish one self-contained "best" theory that will stand out as worthy of a true field of academic study. The result has been the construction of oppositions in which expressivism is relegated to the position of weak "other." (1995, xiv)

As Gradin points out, composition has not realized that romanticism itself constituted a rhetoric and always contained within it the impulses toward democratic action and social critique.

Ross Winterowd's 1992 "Where is English? In the Garden or the Agora?" is another, less well articulated and more stereotypical response to the varying definitions, historical and current, of romanticism and rhetoric in our professional conversation. Winterowd argues that composition, and English studies in general, are in grave danger because they have followed the path of romanticism rather than of rhetoric. He defines romanticism in predictably traditional ways, pointing to its focus on the self, the imagination, and narrative and characterizing its ends as either the "Emersonian ivory tower or Nietzsche's sublunary hell" (1992, 72). In contrast, he offers rhetoric, which he lauds as communicative, communal, public, rigorous, and generous.

In this article, and later in his 1994 *Teacher's Introduction to Composition in the Rhetorical Tradition,* Winterowd not only takes at face value the stereotypical definition of romantic thought, but he uses that definition to demonize it: the emphasis on the self becomes narcissism; the use of narrative becomes navel gazing; the significance of the imagination becomes oppressive elitism. And, as he valorizes the traditional characteristics of rhetoric, he finds that the two stances exist in direct opposition to one another and argues that writing classes, or a profession, cannot afford to accommodate two such conflicting principles, especially when one is destructive to the more important work of the other. In order to make his argument, and because he is caught in the trap of either/or thinking, Winterowd proceeds in traditional fashion, demolishing the opposing claim in order to assert his own. He chooses only one term to investigate honestly—the marketplace, his synonym for rhetoric itself, which he nostalgically discusses as a dying practice. As for the garden, or romantic thought, Winterowd leaves it untouched, except in his assumption that the garden is a wilderness from which any right-thinking English teacher would desire to escape.

Russell's purpose is to create a reinvigorated sense of rhetoric as a discipline cleansed of its associations with messy, ineffectual and elitist romantic thought. Winterowd's purpose is to show how romantic principles, increasingly dominant in English departments, are destroying rhetoric. We think Russell's dichotomy and Winterowd's fear are, first of all, baseless. Romanticism has not dominated and therefore debased rhetoric; moreover, romanticism has never been put into practice systematically in the writing classroom and has never been examined seriously in the history of rhetoric. There are no doubt teachers who have misused personal writing in the composition classroom and who have done a disservice to students by not considering rhetorical contexts or teaching academic discourse. Teachers who encourage only personal story and individual reaction imply that individual vision is unmediated by social and cultural contexts. Much more likely, however, are errors in the other direction where students' experiences and personal investment are always ignored or silenced in favor of public forms. Teachers who focus only on the skills and forms that a system or textbook or curriculum validate neglect the local contexts that determine why, how and if such skills are necessary, as well as the consequences of mastering such skills. In either case, what goes missing is connection—connection among self and other, personal and public— as well as any examination of method, the ways in which writers/ thinkers make the connections, how they observe, act, reflect, and inquire in a developmental process.

The rest of this chapter attempts what Winterowd retreats from and Russell resists: to take a historical look at the romantic "garden" in order to seek out its rhetoric and its method, and thus to show how romanticism and rhetoric have never been in opposition, but have always operated together, and always toward the end of creating a critical, tested faith. Looking at the historical context of romanticism will also allow us to examine the roots of pragmatic philosophy, for both grew out of the earliest days of the colonial experiment in North America. The experimental and practical as well as the transcendent and faithful character of this experiment formed a central part of the cultural myth that influences the thinking of the teachers and philosophers who are affected by this culture.

SEEDS OF ROMANTIC/PRAGMATIC RHETORIC

Romanticism is not an American invention of course, just as romanticism didn't begin in 1798 with Wordsworth's sublime moment as he crossed the Alps. The seeds of romanticism were sown in this country with the settlements of the Puritans, and their experience and philosophy altered the character of the romantic movement in America in the nineteenth century. The ideal of Nature and the importance of the individual took on different—more conscious and rhetorical—dimensions in a land where individuals were required to shape national, as well as individual, identities and where the natural world was as often experienced as a combatant as a refuge. To see American romanticism as completely focused on the individual self is to misread history, to overlook the historical context of the American colonies. The romantic tenets that developed in Puritan/Colonial North America followed from historical circumstance and geographical location as necessary accompaniments to the survival and growth of the colonies. They became—were almost from the first—philosophical principles as well. Freire calls this combination *praxis*. Peirce defines it as *pragmatism*. Both words describe the connection between self and community, belief and action that characterized the attitude of the colonists and the eventual American philosophy that derived from their actions.

This connection has been glossed over in most readings of American intellectual development, especially as individual disciplines use history to explain their own identities. The usual rendering of the history of North American ideas proceeds through metaphors of progress and replacement, with romanticism giving way to pragmatism, pragmatism losing out to modernism, then postmodernism, then post-postmodernism. But that's not the whole story, as we will show by looking again at the most influential and powerful historians of American ideas—Commager, Boorstin, Bercovitch—alongside other, less well known stories. The whole story also includes the powerful tension between individual will and democratic ideals. We look again at large, canonical global histories in order to show that this tension always existed in American philosophy; we put local stories alongside these grand narratives in order to highlight the ways that these tensions played out in lived experience.

What follows is not a linear history, but a reflection that asks what difference it might make to look again, and to look in out of the way places, for a heritage we might be able to use. Susan Griffin, in *The Eros of Everyday Life*, describes the tensions that such a re-examination might uncover.

> As one searches history for the causes of present crises the fear is of the forfeiture of continuity and tradition. But this history is also filled with imprisoned wishes, unrealized dreams, for democracy, a good life, a just society which one can reclaim only by rereading the past. And in the end it is only by the light of continued reflection that continuity and tradition are kept alive. (1995, 30)

And, as Gerda Lerner insists, continuity, tradition, and reflection—including ours—are always local and particular.

THE DOCTRINE OF NECESSITY:
SELF AND COMMUNITY IN DIALOGUE

> Wee shall be as a Citty upon a Hill.
> —John Winthrop, *A Modell of Christian Charity*

The essential difference between American and English romantics lies in the concept of the self. As Sacvan Bercovitch argues, in European romanticism "the ideal centered upon the self-determining, all-embracing individual. Humanity continually circling from the One back to the One" (1985, 36). For North American romantics, in contrast, self from the beginning was created both socially and individually. Americans were, as Stephen Spender says, those "without a past" (quoted in Bercovitch 1985). The present was all, and it had to be forged necessarily in more than individual terms, since part of the project in the New World was making a new world. The circle Bercovitch traces was inscribed in larger and larger arcs, from the one and the other back to the one among others. This "American-ness" of connection accounts in fact for the rhetorical character of American romanticism.

The link between individual and emerging national identity was embodied in the Christian dogma that propelled the Puritans' experiment in Massachusetts. The apostle Paul, primary author of the Puritans' central text, asserts the necessity of connection between self and other in Corinthians in the New Testament, as he characterizes the Christian life: "For just as the body is one and has many members, and all the members of the body, though many, are one body, so it is with Christ" (12:12). Not all the early colonists were Puritans, of course. But even those who settled in New England for economic or social reasons, as did many of the early Pilgrims in the Plimoth Bay Colony, lived the connection between self and other on their own secular terms as they faced the same exigencies of experience and identity that made each person responsible for the community and thus for one another.

The Puritans, however, settling in the port of Boston which was soon to become both thriving and extremely influential in deciding the affairs of an emerging cultural identity, were overt about their religious mission and its social, as well as governmental, implications. Even before the Puritans touched the land of the New World, they were exhorted by their leaders to link individual interests to community endeavor, to subordinate individual concerns to public ones. Aboard the ship *Arbella* in 1630, soon-to-be governor John Winthrop delivered a sermon designed to persuade his travel-weary listeners that success in their endeavor could only be accomplished by merging public and private concern. *A Modell of Christian Charity*, the sermon he preached, is probably the most famous of Winthrop's writings, and in it Winthrop follows out the implications of the apostle Paul's metaphor of the body:

> No body can be perfect which wants its propper ligamentes. All the partes of this body being thus united are made soe contiguous in a speciall relacion as they must needes partake of each others strength and infirmity, joy and sorrow, weale and woe. If one member suffers, all suffer with it; if one be in honour, all rejoyce with it. (1908, 193)

Winthrop suggests that the work at hand in founding a new society was God's work, to be accomplished as a group effort, and only meeting success when self-interested concerns were submerged in the larger concerns of the other's welfare:

> For the worke wee have in hand, it is by a mutuall consent through a speciall overruleing providence, and a more than an ordinary approbation of the Churches of Christ to seeke out a place of Cohabitation and Consorteshipp under a due forme of Government both civill and ecclesiasticall. In such cases as this the care of the publique must oversway all private respects, by which not onely conscience but meare Civill pollicy doth binde us. . . . (196–97)

Many of the most influential American literary histories have shown that the challenges of the land itself meant that whatever philosophy developed would be uniquely different from its European counterparts. The new land and the extraordinary circumstances of beginning a life there meant that old habits and customs might need to be altered, especially the attitudes or customs that concerned self interest:

> We must not content our selves with usuall ordinary meanes; whatsoever wee did or ought to have done when wee lived in england, the same must wee doe and more allsoe where wee goe: . . .we must love one another with a pure hearte fervently; wee must beare one anothers burthens; we must not looke onely on our owne things, but allsoe on the things of our brethren. . . .(197)

For the Puritans, God himself had ordained the establishment of a new venue for his work to be carried out, and, as Winthrop argues, the new circumstances insisted on a new covenant, a new kind of obedience among the group. The settlers had to see their own individual good blended and tied to the good of others in the community:

> For this end, wee must be knitt together in this worke as one man, wee must entertaine each other in brotherly affeccion, wee must be willing to abridge our selves of our superfluities, for the supply of others necessities. We must make others condicions our owne, rejoyce together, mourne together, labour, and suffer together, always having before our eyes our Commission and Community in the worke, our Community as members of the same body. . . . (198)

When Winthrop pleads for a real community in the new land, he's also seeing that community as a symbol of the workings of Providence, an illustration and a lesson to others of God's blessings: "That men shall say of succeeding plantacions: the Lord make it like that of New England." The city was itself then a body, not private but public, an example to be emulated or shunned. If the experiment failed, if resolve weakened, if the colony died out, it would be more than a personal failure; it would serve as a proof to the enemies of God and a shame to all that love God. "All eyes are uponn us," Winthrop warns (198), and the city on the hill must prove itself worthy.

Winthrop's phrase, "Citty on the Hill," symbolizes the dialectical character of personal and public life that was to dominate in New England during the years of its settling and early growth and which becomes a central concept in American romanticism and pragmatism. In the villages and towns in the New England colonies, personal and communal identity merged in daily life and cultural policy. Puritans saw their New World life heuristically; that is, as Bercovitch points out, they viewed it as "the redemptive process at work" both worldwide and within the individual (1985, 34).

One reason that Cotton Mather (1663–1728), perhaps the most influential of the colonial ministers, believed so strongly in the settlement of the new land was that his study of the Bible and his experience in the Colonies convinced him that the colonizing was both fulfillment of prophecy and itself prophetic. According to Bercovitch the Puritan mission of redemption led to this need for prophecy; as Puritans built their communities and at the same time consciously "made history," they continually played out the dialectic between what was and what ought to be. Like most other Puritan ministers, Mather insisted on the public dimension of private experience. The link between private will and public good was often made by locating redemptive properties in the connection. Becoming a symbol for others, working out of common need, recognizing the effects of individual actions—these were all methods for encouraging the dialectic of self/other in the colonial community. The Bible itself was proof to Mather and other Puritan ministers of the connection as requirement for salvation as well as the inescapable nature of private and public. Especially as the Puritans read it, the Bible suggests that nothing can be done in secret, privately, because the Almighty knows every secret thought or action. In its most encompassing sense, then, individuality is always a part of group behavior; the individual is never alone, because his actions always have public consequences.

Two centuries later, Hawthorne writes his greatest novel based on the Puritan realization of the public-ness of the private soul, the community consequences of the will of the individual heart. *The Scarlet Letter* (1850) plays out the moral drama that Mather and others describe in their sermons and letters. One message of *The Scarlet Letter* is the recognition that women, despite the insistence that their role be private rather than public, could act publicly and with community spirit. Hawthorne's Colonial heroine Hester is heroic specifically because she connects private consciousness to public action, as she stands on the town scaffold in public humiliation with private resolution and as she ministers to the needs of her fellow villagers by keeping their secrets as well as healing their ills:

> It will be perceived, too, that, while Hester never put forward even the humblest title to share in the world's privileges,—farther than to breathe the common air, and earn daily bread for little Pearl and herself by the faithful labor of her hands,—she was quick to acknowledge her sisterhood with the race of man, whenever benefits were to be conferred. . . . In all seasons of calamity, indeed, whether general or of individuals, the outcast of society at once found her place. She came, not as a guest, but as a rightful inmate, into the household that was darkened by trouble; as if its gloomy twilight were a medium in which she was entitled to hold intercourse with her fellow-creatures. (1962, 116–17)

Colonial women, like the men of the community, had to alter their positions in the New World. Hester's sin isolates her from the society of her fellows, but her reactions to her isolation are not unrelated to the ways that Colonial women, and men, had to rethink their traditional beliefs and actions in light of the "wilderness" they found themselves in:

> Her intellect and heart had their home, as it were, in desert places, where she roamed as freely as the wild Indian in his woods. For years past she had looked from this estranged point of view at human institutions, and whatever priests or legislators had established; criticizing all with hardly more reverence than the Indian would feel for the clerical band, the judicial robe, the pillory, the gallows,

the fireside, or the church. The tendency of her fate and fortunes had been to set her free. (143)

In a recent historiography, *Good Wives: Image and Reality in the Lives of Women in Northern New England (1650–1750)*, Laurel Thatcher Ulrich demonstrates just how much personal and public life intersected for Colonial women, as well as the freedom that came from the novel situations in which they found themselves. By examining the occasional court records, family letters, and journals, and by reading gravestones, Ulrich illuminates the lives of women whose stories were mostly hidden. What Ulrich finds is the kind of strong, independent woman that Hester Prynne represents—women who buy and sell property, who take care of community as well as domestic business, who help determine religious and secular activities—in other words, who act in ways that link private and public action. "Fate and fortune," as Hawthorne puts it, combined to make women move from traditional private spheres into new, mediated, ones.

The Puritan Dorothy Dudley's life is a case in point. When she died in Boston in 1643, her gravestone told her virtues. She was "eminent for holiness, prayerfulness, watchfulness, zeal, prudence, sincerity, humility, meekness, patience, weanedness from the world, self denial, publick spiritedness, diligence, faithfulness and charity" (Ulrich 1982, 3). But Dorothy Dudley's virtues were not hers alone: Ulrich finds them repeated on stone after stone, and she notes that preachers used the same words to exhort their congregations in sermon after sermon across New England during the first hundred years of its settling. The implication of communal personality is strange to consider, especially in a culture that invests so much in the cult of individualism. As Ulrich says, "It is difficult for us [readers] to approach a world in which neither innovation nor individual was celebrated. . . . Yet the purpose of an epitaph was not to commemorate but to transcend personality" (36).

To "transcend personality" meant not so much losing individuality as it did grounding individuality in the community at large. The virtues written on the gravestones of women and men who lived in the colonies were the virtues the colonies needed for their continuance, and the merging or submerging of the self within the public sphere was a primary characteristic of Puritan life.

Contingency as Practice and Principle

A—In Adam's fall
We sinned all.

Y—Youth forward slips
Death soonest nips.

—New England Primer

For the experiment of life in a new world to be carried out success-fully, and for the colonists to understand the deep need for individual and community interests to become tied together, teaching became a necessary tool. In colonial communities, literacy was linked not only to religious principle, but to the more practical end of establishing a method for preservation and enhancement of the colony.

Children in New England learned their letters by learning to "read" the signs of their culture as well, the elements that connected and distinguished their lives in the wilderness from the more stable lives their parents had led in the Old World. Much of the *Bay Psalm Book* (1640) as well as the *New England Primer* (1683) focused on the teaching of letters with the aim of salvation, reached by inculcating Protestant theology, in mind. "In Adam's fall/We sinned all" told Puritan children that they began life in sin and error as fallen beings, the heirs of Adam's bad decision. The story of Adam told Puritan schoolchildren of the importance of a single life, its potential conse-quences for all as well as of their need—inborn—for redemption from Adam's sin. The whole Protestant impulse toward literacy was thus doctrinal and devoutly anti-Catholic as well, a statement against the infallibility of any human priest or pope, and the consequent neces-sity for each person to learn for himself the law of God, and find salvation himself, not trusting in other men as substitutes for divine authority.

"Youth forward slips/Death soonest nips" reminded the Puritans of a lesson both temporal and spiritual, especially meaningful to their uncertain lives in a land surrounded by named and unnamed dangers. While death was a part of human existence everywhere and so the need to live a life to redeem Adam's sin was crucial, in the new land with its strange and more potent dangers it was a daily ever-present fear. Neither personal nor community existence could be taken for granted; both were demonstrably fragile. Personal life and community endeavor had to remain ready for change, had to take advantage of chance when it presented itself. Since few things could be depended upon, life had to be more or less made up. Death's hovering presence accounted for what Ulrich finds a characteristic of early New Englanders, their intense anxiety about the community they were in the process of establishing. "New Englanders," she notes, "had a deep fear of social disintegration. They cherished stability even when they could not attain it" (1982, 154).

The threat of extermination by disease or starvation or cold or intruder was always present for the early settlers. The village was held together by its religious hope for a better world and a belief in the rightness of its mission. It was also strengthened by a hard-headed practicality derived from the realization that any stability arising from hope or from confidence couldn't be attained completely or for long. Half the Pilgrims died in Plymouth the first year, and even established villages were subject at any time to devastating disease as well as raids from outraged native tribes. In such extreme conditions, old verities and traditions didn't necessarily hold up or help.

William Bradford, first governor of the Plimoth Bay Colony, gives a moving account of the first winter in Plymouth that shows how tenuous the hold was on the land in its early settling:

> But that which was most sad and lamentable was, that in two or three months' time half of their company died, especially in January and February. . . . So as there died some times two or three of a day in the foresaid time, that of 100 and odd persons, scarce fifty remained. And of these, in the time of most distress, there was but six or seven sound persons who to their great commendations, be it spoken, spared no pains night nor day, but with abundance of toil and hazard of their own health, fetched them wood, made them fires, dressed them neat, made their beds, washed their loathsome clothes, clothed and unclothed them. In a word, did all of the homely and necessary offices for them which dainty and queasy stomachs cannot endure to hear named; and all this willingly and cheerfully, without any grudging in the least showing herein their true love unto their friends and brethren; a rare example and worthy to be remembered. (1990, 218)

The men and women of Plimoth Plantation acted according to what Winthrop called a new covenant, submerging for the sake of survival the personal within the community good, preparing themselves to adapt and adopt new habits of mind. The fragility of their enterprise as a community was mirrored in the brevity of their own individual lives. And such fragility lent practical support to the need for a systematic working out of the principles of individual will and public need. What the pragmatist Peirce was to call at the end of the nineteenth century the "doctrine of use" intertwined in the early colonial settlements with their strong sense of mission and of faith.

"STRANGELY DID THE LORD PROVIDE FOR THEM": THE NECESSITY OF EXPERIMENT

Life in the colonies, including religious life, had to change from accepted tradition. Old ways had to accommodate to new circumstances. Historian Daniel Boorstin points out that the belief in community itself, the recognition of how public life imposed itself upon private consciousness, grew from what he calls a "uniquely American" condition (1958, 10). Unlike in Europe, in the colonial village there was no class or group of assigned individuals whose function was to supply answers to community questions, no special class of university-educated, moneyed, titled men to set policy and enlighten others. Consequently, the group and the individual endeavor was from the first a matter of experimentation rather than preordained rule. This was so even among the Puritans, who believed Truth had been given to them in the Word of God. Life in the New World required that the early colonists examine closely and question in practical ways what they might have accepted unquestioningly in their already-established European towns. The apostle Paul's admonition to "work out your own salvation" became a guiding principle for the new inhabitants of the continent.

The necessity for experiment rather than tradition to guide behavior was nowhere more evident than in the position of early Colonial women. Colonial women took on new roles in village and wilderness, acting as husbands' deputies in their absence, helping to build communities and defend life and property when occasion demanded.

Ulrich documents cases of women who turned away robbers, rescued cattle, and in one dramatic case, returned from captivity with scalps as proof of the determination to settle the land. Some took the law into their own hands to punish intruders who had raided their villages.

Women's unique position in the new land meant that in early settlements they were not exempt from helping make policy, from having a public—as well as domestic—effect on the life of the village. Mary Rowlandson was a Colonial woman whose ability to improvise and whose strength of purpose were tested in a terrible ordeal where she was taken captive in a Wampanoag Indian raid on the Lancaster settlement west of Boston in 1675. Rowlandson's account of the raid, her kidnapping and imprisonment and her eventual restoration to her family became one of the most popular works of the seventeenth century. Published in 1682 after her death in 1678, the story is one of the first captivity narratives. Rowlandson laments both her condition and her own lack of faith, learns how to survive and adapt, and eventually finds solace as she comes to believe that the captivity is a test of her worthiness to become one of God's chosen. Rowlandson's account of her life as a Puritan woman and a representative of the "city on the hill" exposes the workings of Puritan consciousness within the framework of early American life in a land and among people they had little ability to understand.

Rowlandson writes in careful detail about the lives of her captors. The "savage heathens" are viewed as the time and her religion would have taught her to see them. When the Wampanoags perform small kind acts, like offering a piece of meat to her, she sees not their kindness but only God's providence working through the devil's agents. She wonders at God's forbearance in keeping the Indian alive in the wilderness. "Strangely," she notes, "did the Lord provide for them" (1990, 325). Like most colonists of her day, Rowlandson finds mostly savagery in the culture she observes. It would have been hard for her not to claim savagery, given the way she had come in contact with the tribe when seventeen of her family and friends had been killed. "Thus were we butchered by those merciless heathen, standing amazed, with the blood running down to our heels" (319). But her reaction to her captors is also a part of her Puritan ideology. As historian Garry Wills points out, the treatment of the inhabitants the Puritans encountered in America was colored by a belief in the active workings on earth of the Antichrist, and thus the need to colonize the world for God, a condition that the imminently expected Second Coming mandated. The Puritan was constantly tested and imperiled in doing the work of the Lord. "The Indians," notes Wills, "instruments of the devil, were being used to try the saints and to undo God's work. Even friendly overtures were likely to be part of a larger strategy to disarm the Christians . . ." (1990, 140).

Still, despite her fear and contempt, Rowlandson finds herself unable to dismiss her interest in and her questions about the people she lives with for over a year. Rowlandson questions God's providence when the Indians find food in unexpected locations or escape from a troop of colonials, and wonders at their unexpected kindness in bringing her a Bible to read or demonstrating community spirit:

> There one of them asked me, why I wept, I could hardly tell what to say: yet I answered, they would kill me: No, said he, none will hurt you. Then came one of them and gave me two spoon-fulls of Meal to comfort me, and another gave me half a pint of Pease; which was more worth than many Bushels at another time. (1990, 327)

Comprehending that the Wampanoags shared rations at cost to their own well-being, Rowlandson still doesn't rethink her cultural conditioning or the strong dicta that hold her Puritan community together. But she does begin to observe and think rather than simply accept; she speaks rather than listens as she speculates on the lives of the members of the tribe, drawing conclusions that help her to make sense of her ordeal. She makes her captivity a process of redemption and understanding; when the Indians become agents in her own repentance, their acts make them—at least for the moment—God's creatures: "Affliction I wanted, and affliction I had, full measure pressed down and running over; yet I see, when God calls a Person to any thing, and through never so many difficulties, yet he is fully able to carry them through and make them see, and say they have been the gainers thereby (341).

Had she been able to expand her perspective a little further, she might have seen a compatriot among her guards, the princess Weetamoo, who helped lead the Wampanoag tribe along with her husband and whose skills and survival strategies matched Rowlandson's own. Weetamoo is the "mistress" Rowlandson speaks of who gives her food and who seems to Rowlandson so unyielding. Her story is both brave and tragic, as she created innovative strategies to keep her people alive and to drive the colonists away. She managed to elude the British again and again and keep her tribe from starving for a long time until she was finally caught. She and her children were sold into slavery in the West Indies, and Weetamoo died trying to escape. Although Rowlandson is deeply afraid of her captors, she is respectful of Weetamoo's power and notes with awe Weetamoo's dignity: "a severe and proud Dame she was . . . dressing herself as neat as much time as any of the Gentry in the land" (332). Weetamoo was powerful and proud, a Sachem or chief of her tribe, and from many accounts a brilliant leader. Like Rowlandson herself, could they both have but known it, Weetamoo employed the doctrine of use in order to help her people.

Rowlandson was a good Puritan, and Puritans of course believed in Truth—their theology taught them that Truth was waiting to be discovered by the vigilant and faithful. And they believed that the Lord had decided who was to know truth and who it was to be hidden from. But methods for finding truth varied between the world of settled city and emerging village. Mary Rowlandson considered herself one of the elect, one chosen to know, because of her trial in captivity; the Plimoth Pilgrims spoke of locating truth as they nursed their friends out of illnesses; Jonathan Edwards, like Emerson a hundred years later, understood truth in encountering the natural world. The way toward knowledge, it seemed, was not pre-established in form, even if it appeared to be in content. Henry Steele Commager links North Americans' understanding of truth to their physical setting, which made them inclined toward process, ingenuity, and change. In describing the way the emerging country built its settlements, he notes the "unfinished quality" of the villages, suggesting impermanence and thus partial, not complete, knowledge (1950, 18).

This experimental quality of truth comes from what Commager believes to be a deep practicality embedded in the American character. "Philosophy," Commager explains, is to the American "the resort of the unhappy and the bewildered, and the American knew he was neither" (5). This stance explains the inclination among the early settlers and later generations of Americans to experiment, to emphasize process and use. Commager continues: "Neither Transcendentalism nor pragmatism, the two ways of thinking that can properly be designated American, had a systematic quality and it was suggestive that [North America's] most characteristic form of philosophy, pragmatism, should emphasize the unfinished nature of the universe" (18).

Rowlandson's account demonstrates this relationship between truth and context, showing how tentative ideas needed to remain if one were to survive, much less prosper. "I had often before this said," writes Rowlandson with moving frankness, "that if the Indians should come, I should chuse rather to be killed by them then taken alive but when it came to the tryal my mind changed; their glittering weapons so daunted my spirit, that I chose rather to go along with those (as I may say) ravenous Beasts, then that moment to end my days" (1990, 320). Rowlandson's practical spirit overcame her fear and led her to nurse herself, locate strengths and abilities to help her survive and be of use to her captors, accomplishing many things—like discussions with her captors that led eventually to her release—that could happen only with a determined willingness to adapt to change.

The idea of tentativeness, or experimentation, began in the practical need of colonists like Rowlandson, but became by Revolutionary War times an ideal American quality. The cliché "Yankee ingenuity" is a mark of how closely associated the characteristic of empirical inquiry was with American thought and action. Benjamin Franklin, writing a generation after Rowlandson, is a spectacular case in point of the virtues of the experimental and the pragmatic. His individual success as inventor, printer, statesman, and writer became for generations of Americans a metaphor for the potential success of the American experiment itself, not an aberrant individual story but a possible narrative for all Americans who had—to quote Horatio Alger— pluck and luck. Franklin's American tale is a testament to the benefits that derive from freedom and responsibility—for being given the right and the duty to become an observer and a knower.

Franklin writes about that double duty of freedom and responsibility in *The Autobiography* as well as in many of the articles he printed in *Poor Richard's Almanac*. In "Information to Those Who Would Remove to America," Franklin gives would-be émigrés a list of advantages and responsibilities of life in the New World:

> [T]olerable good Workmen in any of those mechanic arts are sure to find Employ, and to be well paid for their Work, there being no Restraints preventing Strangers from exercising any Art they

understand, nor any Permission necessary. If they are poor, they begin first as Servants or Journeymen; and if they are sober, industrious, and frugal, they soon become Masters, establish themselves in Business, marry, raise Families and become respectable Citizens. (1990, 812)

Franklin establishes both the ideal of American virtue and the method of achieving it. Practicality, situation-dependent action and belief, community, and individual will were the hallmarks of ideal American character.

The role of the community in establishing ingenuity and experimentation as values is as clear in Franklin's life and work as in Rowlandson's account. Daniel Boorstin shows how the formation of groups in this country proceeded from necessity, since no established groups dictated matters of policy to the rest. Puritan theology sanctioned the group, since groups underscored the belief in the role of individual responsibility and public action as essentially the same. The seeming paradox of individual recognition in group endeavor is erased with the Puritan understanding of public will as an extension of private act. Henry Steele Commager points out the connection as he speaks of more contemporary Americans: "For all his individualism, the American was much given to cooperative undertakings and to joining. As the American had created his church and his state, he took for granted his capacity to create all lesser institutions and associations" (1950, 22). The American, as Commager describes him, can join groups because they form an extension of his own individualistic ideas. Like Whitman, who claims in *Song of Myself* that "Every atom belonging to me as good as belongs to you," the American makes sharing an individual and group project.

Ann Ruggles Gere's book on the development of writing groups underscores the point made by Boorstin and Commager. She finds that noninstitutional groups (those not constituted formally in academic settings) established themselves based on two principles or impulses: an egalitarian view of knowledge and a social view of the method for making knowledge. Gere uses the term "American" to describe these impulses toward groups, the democratic belief that anyone could—needed to be, in fact—a knower, and that banding together to *know* enhanced both the rate and effect of change on the larger community (1987, 33–35). Groups, she argues, are most effective when they meet for real purposes that they themselves define, and these purposes are both practical and ideal; that is, they are designed in terms of use and spiritual need. Gere's study examines the development of women's writing groups, and her overall point underscores Boorstin's and Commager's descriptions of the American impulse toward community, not a gender-specific male desire to exclude women, nor an exclusively female need to band together to gain power, but a result of the uniquely American tension between self and other.

The dynamic role of groups, as Gere describes them, and their dialectical purpose—to establish community and individual identity—define two philosophical positions that help characterize romantic/pragmatic rhetoric: the belief in the individual knower as potential truth-finder and the belief that the methods and the outcomes of knowing were the property of everyone. These beliefs together led to a communal spirit that characterized the conversion narratives, the journals and letters, as well as the government documents, in the early settlements.

From the very first, the "pragmatic"—use, context, experiment—and the "romantic"—faith, individuality, prophecy—intertwine in the American experience. This dialogue of vision and action, and insistence on the dialectical nature of each separately as well as together, is not any kind of linear move from one world view to another. It's clear that the Puritans sowed the seeds of romantic/pragmatic rhetoric that were to ripen in the thought of the great American romantics, Emerson, Thoreau, Hawthorne, and others. Emerson's "new man" disembarked from the *Arbella* and the *Mayflower* prepared to do new work on the continent. The prophetic vision that informed Puritan action and belief consequently became a part of American romanticism's and pragmatism's most important features. And it's prophecy that most strongly makes the link to rhetoric, for prophecy insists on communication between knower and inquirer and implies a communication of belief that might initiate change.

Cornel West today calls his own philosophy "prophetic pragmatism," and he names four elements of this "prophetic thought": (1) discernment: "a broad and deep analytical grasp of the present in light of the past"; (2) connection: or human empathy, "never losing sight of the humanity of others"; (3) tracking hypocrisy: "accenting boldly, and defiantly, the gap between principles and practice"; and (4) hope: "keep alive the notion . . . that the future is open-ended and that what we think and what we do can make a difference" (1993b, 3–7). Belief and action tied together also constitute Freire's definition of *praxis,* the method he advocates for effecting societal change. The significance of context, the need for the experimental, the realization of private and public connection, the role of communal effort, and the belief in truth as possible outcome were the hallmarks of the thought of the Puritans and other early settlers. Those tenets were carried into the nineteenth and twentieth centuries in the two philosophical enterprises Commager identifies as uniquely American: transcendental romanticism and pragmatism.

THREE

ROMANTIC DIALECTICS AND THE PRINCIPLE OF MEDIATION

> Trust thyself; every heart beats to that iron string.
> —Ralph Waldo Emerson, "The American Scholar"

> Our project is not the destruction of the machine but the humanization of man.
> —Paulo Freire, *Education for Critical Consciousness*

The Puritan vision of North America, at once prophetic and experimental, individual and communal, remained a part of the central American philosophical position long after Puritan theology had been officially abandoned. Eventually, Puritan religion and the rise of democratic politics combined to create a brand of romanticism that differed radically from its European version. Emerson, the developer, popularizer, and apologist for the romantic tradition in this country, wrote "The American Scholar" in 1837 as a manifesto for a new way of thinking that would separate the work of thinkers in America from their European counterparts. Where Wordsworth reconstituted a world within himself, Emerson makes himself in the "American Scholar" the "harbinger of a nation designed to fill the postponed expectations of the world" (52). Emerson becomes the representative of this new vision, as Sacvan Bercovitch points out, not its unique expounder, and he can bypass specifics of his historical and personal condition because he is but one among many (1985, 37).

Emerson is the dominant figure in American romanticism, and, as Cornel West asserts in *The American Evasion of Philosophy*, the writer who prefigures most clearly the dominant themes of American pragmatism. Emerson's romanticism meant that he took his ideals for realities, believed them to be part of real and possible action. In short, as West says, Emerson made principles and practices combine as he argued for "some kind of inseparable link between thought and action, theory and practice" (1989, 10). If this connection, called "romantic" by West and "pragmatic" by James, sounds much like modern-day theories of literacy like Freire's and Vygotsky's, the link is not accidental. Emerson foreshadows not only the pragmatism of Peirce, James, Dewey, and others, but the studies of cognition and literacy that have influenced composition studies so profoundly in the last thirty years.

Yet, although Emerson's work has deep connections to the work of these theorists and others whose work might be called (but has not been) romantic or pragmatic, he has often been confined critically to a niche that would make of him the embodiment of one of his most famous essays, "Self-Reliance" (1841). In this essay, Emerson seems to establish himself not as the progenitor for such democratic and liberationist thinkers as Freire but as the patriarch for the great "captains of industry," the robber barons who used a doctrine of individual success to justify their rapacious self-interest. "We must go alone," he claims. "Why should we assume the faults of our friend, or wife, or father, or child, because they sit around our hearth, or are said to have the same blood?" (1969c, 85); and "Be it known unto you henceforward I obey no law less than eternal law . . . I will not hide my tastes or aversions" (85). Even his earliest and probably most important essay, "Nature" (1834), classifies the ways in which the natural world benefits humans and thus seems to lend support to the idea of the ugly American, who takes from the land or the powerless what he needs to prosper and claims it as an American ideal.

But if he's open to the charge that his work has been used to support unrestrained capitalism or unethical individualism, it is no less true that Emerson's rhetoric and purpose oppose such applications. In "Self-Reliance," for example, the assertions of selfhood and individual will are followed by a statement that shows how clearly Emerson recognized the wrongheaded uses his program might be put to: "The populace think that your rejection of popular standards is a rejection of all standard, and mere antinomianism; and the bold sensualist will use the name of philosophy to gild his crimes" (1969c, 86). The response to this misappropriation is for Emerson, as it is for Freire, critical consciousness. "But the law of consciousness abides," Emerson continues: "Consider whether you have satisfied your duties to father, mother, cousin, neighbor, town, cat and dog. . . . But I may also neglect this reflex standard and absolve me to myself" (86). Consciousness—understanding one's responsibilities to self and other—teaches truth. And West points out that Emerson's musings on power, from the publication of "The American Scholar" on, indicate an awareness of social and cultural imbalance that many traditional critics ignore. Emerson does believe strongly in the power of individuals: "In yourself slumbers the whole of Reason; it is for you to know all, it is for you to dare all" (1969a, 55). But the powers of individuals are not separable from the powers of the group, of the culture in which the individual resides: "A nation of men will for the first time exist, because each believes himself inspired by the Divine Soul which also inspires all men" (55).

It's this connection between individual consciousness and national or public change and growth that Emerson stresses even in "Self-Reliance," the essay that may have been the Bible for the soon-to-be millionaires Rockefeller and Carnegie and Gould. Although Emerson spoke to a Harvard elite when he delivered "The American Scholar" and many of his other speeches, his words opened, rather than closed, possibilities for social change. But the social message, this recognition of social inequity and the need for change, was implicit rather than overt. It took pragmatism, especially the philosophy of Dewey, to define explicitly a vision of social change based on a realization of the power of mainstream culture that Emerson only alluded to. Emerson was too willing to see the oppressed as merely those who were unconscious of power or of their own potential, too little able to recognize that powerlessness itself prevented consciousness. Nevertheless, Emerson's enormous effect on American culture and ideology needs to be investigated in terms of its pragmatic, social, and contingent character as much as it has been on its individual and optimistic tenets.

Emerson's ideas owe much to the Puritans, but it's not hard to hear echoes of Emerson in the generation of writers directly preceding his work. Writers before Emerson had used the notion of escape from European influence to identify their new cultural self-definition. The Declaration of Independence itself is a document that reflects many of the principles the Puritans embraced—the imposition of private in public affairs, the role of the group in creating meaning, the primacy given circumstance. Its rhetoric—and its incipient romanticism—is one reason James Kinneavy calls the Declaration an example of "public expressive" discourse (1971, 409).

James Fenimore Cooper, Washington Irving, and others had at the beginning of the century followed a romantic path in their depiction of countryside as a receding past. The nostalgia associated with some romantic thought is evident in the depiction of the almost-archaic Natty Bumppo and the literally archaic Rip Van Winkle. Both these writers, however, follow the European path rather than forge a new American one. Both avid readers of Scott and devotees of European manners, Cooper takes little advantage of the new land even as he describes it in such living detail, and Irving creates characters who, though American, retain European style and sensibility.

It remained for Emerson, his colleagues and followers to elucidate the romantic position as it pertained to the North American experiment. The readers of Coleridge and Wordsworth and the grandchildren of Puritans and Pilgrims in the wilderness developed a new kind of romantic thought that linked itself inextricably to practice and context. Emerson's view of knowledge is radically different from European conceptions, interested not in justifying a set of representations or reifying static categories but in seeking to examine consciousness and change itself. Modern European philosophy was for Emerson static and outdated relative to the tasks he chose for himself. His language is tentative—"All language is vehicular and transitive, and is good, as ferries and horses are, for conveyance, not as farms and houses are, for homestead" (1969b, 382)—and his emphasis is on possibility, use, tactic, rather than on a quest for certainty or foundations. This is why West sees in Emerson the pragmatist's agenda; his refusal to accept the primary tenets of European philosophy since they were inappropriate to his interests—his *evasion* of modern philosophy, as West puts it—makes him the protopragmatist. As West says, "this distinctly American refusal is the crucible from which emerge the sensibilities and sentiments of future American pragmatists" (1993a, 36).

SELF-RELIANCE AND COMMUNITY RESPONSIBILITY

> The deeper he dives into his privatest, secretest presentiment, to his wonder he finds this is the most acceptable, most public, and universally true.
>
> —Emerson, "American Scholar"

In American romantic/pragmatic rhetoric a guiding principle is the uniting of dualisms. Especially is this so in Emerson's thought as he teases out the paradoxes contained in "unity in multeity," Coleridge's romantic phrase (136). Self-reliance itself builds upon that paradox, that one finds community in self and self in community. The simultaneous inward and outward search is a function of rhetoric, of knowing the self in order to know others and understanding others in order to understand the world inhabited by the self. And it's deeply a part of American romanticism, steeped in the inward turning of religious thought and outward yearning for a new community where such thoughts are given nourishment.

Interestingly, little of the personal self emerges in Emerson's writing, just as little of the autobiographical self finds a place in Whitman's *Song of Myself* or as little of the intimate is revealed in Thoreau's narrative of his two years spent at Walden Pond. These romantic writers seldom record an individual communion with nature or the struggling for communion to benefit the soul. For the most part, they teach a *method* for communing, as though the solitary personal struggle is at one with other personal struggles. This is indeed how American romantic/pragmatic rhetoricians dissolve the dichotomy the Europeans seem to embrace by considering the self's relationship to society. The self is always part of a larger self, determined by but also determining that larger self. "What I assume you shall assume," Whitman says confidently at the opening to *Song of Myself:* "For every atom of me as good as belongs to you" (line 2,727). The American romantic's notion of the self as representative and social rather than unique and isolated is a conception of self closer to Vygotsky than to Wordsworth.

The knowledge of self that might ensue from an investigation into the connection between an individual and the natural world that surrounded him does not finish the task for the American romantics. As Emerson and Thoreau and others make clear, to know the self is to

know how to know others. In *Nature*, his hymn to personal communion and knowledge of self through nature, Emerson places himself not
in a wilderness or even at Walden Pond, but in the middle of Boston
Common, surrounded by the signs of New England community in
the nineteenth century, livestock and beggars, the lights from cottages
and hostels, the sound of horses in the street. His "transparent eye-
ball"—"I am nothing; I see all"—then, looks not only inward, or upward, but outward to the world of the Common. In "The American
Scholar," which is often read and taught as Emerson's hymn to American individual self-reliance, Emerson writes: "The poet, in utter soli-
tude, remembering his spontaneous thoughts and recording them, is
found to have recorded that which men in crowded cities find true for
them also . . . that they drink his word because he fulfills for them their
own nature . . ." (1969a, 59). The self does more than link itself through
introspection to society; the knowledge of self attained in the process
of self-examination becomes a lesson on how to be a self in a world
populated by other selves.

Emerson isn't the only one of the American romantics to be taught
in school as the primary proponent of self above all, or self in opposition to society. In fact, Thoreau is used even more frequently to symbolize the romantic vision of the isolated and egoistic poet, retreating
from a world that prevents self-knowledge. It's Thoreau, after all, who
takes Emerson's prescription in "The American Scholar" to heart and
retreats to Walden Pond to become "man thinking." Thoreau's experience as he relates it in *Walden* is, in fact, not primarily isolated or self-
involved, but communal and dialectical. Thoreau as often muses about
the world as he does about himself, and he describes the social world
that exists in nature in more detail than he does his own consciousness. When he observes the pond during the seasons, he often sees it
in relation to the railroad that borders it; when he describes his house
or the woods he often speaks of the visitors who teach him how he's
understanding the connection of one person to another and to the
world. *Walden* is a pragmatic experiment, not a merely romantic retreat or story, testing theory and suggesting a program for possible
action; and it's important to remember that Thoreau's purpose in this
work is rhetorical, not merely reflective. Thoreau's deliberate com-
pression of two years' experience into one where each season represents an evolution of understanding shows that the aim is to teach and
persuade as much as to describe. The imperatives in his syntax—"Sim-

plify, simplify"—are not chants but messages, tentative hypotheses and conclusions, suggestions to his friends and readers.

Walden is most often read as a kind of European romanticism, the familiar retreat from a corrupt society and the move toward a pure and unpeopled nature. However, Thoreau's is an American romantic/pragmatic rhetorical vision—a socially activist method and suggestion for how to live in the world, not a passivist retreat from the world. At the beginning of the book, Thoreau compares his book to a coat that readers are invited to try on. "Perhaps these pages are more particularly addressed to poor students. As for the rest of my readers, they will accept such portions as apply to them. I trust that none will stretch the seams in putting on the coat, for it may do good service to him whom it fits" (1966, 1–2). Thoreau's purpose is to change his world, the world of an increasingly "progressive" America where he finds his fellows "doing penance in a thousand remarkable ways," in their enslavement to idea of growth, and to their need to possess goods. Slavery itself is a theme Thoreau uses literally and metaphorically here in *Walden* (1854), indicating his awareness of its social evil and alluding to his more overt social statement in *On Civil Disobedience* (1849):

> I sometimes wonder that we can be so frivolous, I may almost say, as to attend to the gross but somewhat foreign form of servitude called Negro Slavery, there are so many keen and subtle masters that enslave both north and south. . . . Look at the teamster on the highway, wending to market by day or night, does any divinity stir within him? His highest duty to fodder and water his horses! What is his destiny to him compared with the shipping interests? Does not he drive for Squire Make-a-Stir? How godlike, how immortal, is he? See how he cowers and sneaks, how vaguely all the day he fears, not being immortal nor divine, but the slave and prisoner of his own opinion of himself, a fame won by his own deeds. (1966, 4–5)

Thoreau uses the elevated and hortatory rhetoric of the preacher throughout *Walden* as a way to encourage and chide his reader, who, Thoreau clearly has decided, should try on and fit into the coat he's offering.

The North American romantics wrestled with the conflicts they experienced between retreat and engagement in the world. They sought to challenge and rethink arguments about faith and science, democracy and elitism, and between public and private agendas. David Reynolds's book, *Beneath the American Renaissance: The Subversive Imagination in the Age of Emerson and Melville*, shows how the popular texts of reform literature and local-color writing contributed to an understanding of these conflicts in the work of the "major" American romantics: "The use [these] figures made of sensational literature, moral reform, and Puritan religion exposed dualism in American society—democratic but slave-holding, open country but with teeming cities, etc., with an outward innocence but an inward demonism" (1988, 79).

But as the American romantics confronted the dualism in American culture they exposed something else besides, a mediating or third principle that forced writers to remake or reconcile the either/or conflicts they observed. Emerson's meditation on intention and action from his *Journal* exemplifies this kind of rethinking: "He who has only good intention is apt to feel ashamed of his inaction and slightness of his virtue when in the presence of active and zealous leaders of the philanthropic enterprises of Universal temperance, Peace and Abolition of Slavery" (quoted in Reynolds 1988, 45). But as Reynolds shows, Emerson reaches an understanding of how his writing functions as both reflection and action, at once subverting traditional order and creatively reconstituting it. Emerson's writing, in other words, becomes his reform action and allows him to work within the tension of word and deed.

THE RHETORIC OF ROMANTICISM

Despite its attempts to persuade readers to a new vision of consciousness and change, *Walden*, like Emerson's work, is still most often taught as a treatise on the virtues of individuality and self-reliance, on the innocence of Nature and the pleasures of the hermetic life. The dialectical and pragmatic character of *Walden* is ignored by critics, readers, and teachers, and it's easy to see how American romanticism can be ignored or declared passé as well, for romanticism is taught the way *Walden* is: as a literary period that celebrated the ego, nature, and retreat from the world without recognizing romanticism's dialectical, rhetorical nature or its social purposes. When teaching and theory organize philosophical history into categories, usually in categories of opposition, hierarchy, or linearity, readers can easily forget the philosophical position that guided the writing of both *Walden* and *On Civil Disobedience*. It's even more difficult to recognize, trace, and teach the connections to current thinkers and teachers who inherit and practice the same romantic/pragmatic rhetoric as Emerson, Thoreau, James, and Dewey. As we will show in the following chapters, many twentieth-century philosophers and teachers, Paulo Freire among them, practice romantic/pragmatic rhetoric and yet suffer from the pejorative half-label "romantic" because our intellectual and disciplinary history is described in linear evolutionary stages that deny overlap, continuity, and interweaving among ideas across time and space, and the uses of the past.

The rhetoric employed by the romantics is one that makes use of self-discovery as a tool for societal recovery and change. Thoreau issues a disingenuous apology at the beginning of *Walden* for his use of the self:

> In most books, the *I*, or first person, is omitted; in this it will be retained; that, in respect to egotism, is the main difference. We commonly do not remember that it is, after all, always the first person that is speaking. I should not talk so much of myself if there were anybody else whom I knew as well. (1966, 1)

This narrative of self-discovery becomes for romantic/pragmatic rhetoricians a most powerful persuasive tool, given their insistence that experience is always at once connected and unique; one person's life confronts and connects to another's.

The story of a self would seem far from the work of some of the recent theorists we have been calling romantic/pragmatic rhetoricians. Freire's philosophical design, for example, seems to deny the single narrative in favor of creating a method for rethinking a world that places some groups on the margins without power or voice. But like Thoreau and Emerson, Freire's liberatory pedagogy begins in self-discovery, as he suggests in *Education for Critical Consciousness*: "The important thing is to help men (and nations) help themselves, to place them in consciously critical confrontation with their problems, to make them the agents of their own recuperation" (1990, 16). In his 1980 work, *Literacy: Reading the Word and the World*, Freire uses his own story of literacy, how he learned the signs of his culture and then the words, as a way to advocate a theory of literacy and of consciousness. In all of

Freire's work, the understanding of the ways marginal or powerless people in a society come to consciousness and action proceeds from the use of personal experience as a frame of reference for social critique and action.

Freire's discussion of the oppressed is echoed by two romantic/pragmatic writers in nineteenth-century America who, themselves on the margins of their cultures and determined to change those cultures, use personal and public narrative in much the same way that Freire does. When Frederick Douglass writes his *Narrative* he makes a similar case for the public relevance and revolutionary usefulness of self-initiation and discovery. The entire autobiography is an argument for the abolition of slavery, of course, but it is also a powerful statement that takes the romantic position of self-awareness as a method toward societal change. In this section, for example, the famous learning-to-read scene, Douglass discovers how the individual case provokes societal awareness:

> Very soon after I went to live with Mr. and Mrs. Auld, she very kindly commenced to teach me the A, B, C. After I had learned this, she assisted me in learning to spell words of three or four letters. Just at this point of my progress, Mr. Auld found out what was going on, and at once forbade Mrs. Auld to instruct me further, telling her, among other things, that it was unlawful, as well as unsafe, to teach a slave to read. . . . "Now, said he, if you teach that nigger (speaking of myself) how to read, there would be no keeping him. It would forever unfit him to be a slave. He would at once become unmanageable, and of no value to his master. As to himself, it could do him no good, but a great deal of harm. It would make him discontented and unhappy." These words sank deep into my heart, stirred up by sentiments within that lay slumbering, and called into existence an entirely new train of thought. It was a new and special revelation, explaining dark and mysterious things, with which my youthful understanding had struggled, but struggled in vain. I now understood what had been to me a most perplexing difficulty—to wit, the white man's power to enslave the black man. It was a grand achievement and I prized it highly. From that moment, I understood the pathway from slavery to freedom. (1963, 36)

Douglass's entire account is an eloquent testimony to the ways in which personal narrative becomes symbolic account. Douglass is clear about his experiences standing for rather than against his fellow sufferers. The individual experience, as he writes it, is an instance that one can use as proof for an argument. William Lloyd Garrison, Douglass's champion, indicates in the Preface to the *Narrative* the power of the personal statement toward public, persuasive ends: "Who can read that passage, and be insensible to its pathos and sublimity? Compressed into it is a whole Alexandrian library of thought, feeling and sentiment—all that can, all that need be urged, in the form of expostulation, entreaty, rebuke against that crime of crimes—making man the property of his fellow-man!" (1963, xv–xvi). Douglass makes the narrative-as-symbol an argument about the tragic paradox of slaves in a democratic society. As Garrison frames the narrative, the Douglass story becomes a call to action and a method for change; Garrison's word "insensible" means more than "mere feeling." For Garrison— abolitionist/activist—to be "sensible" is to act. Douglass's appeal is to common humanity and to decency as much as to patriotism, and his own best argument is himself, whether standing before a group or writing in powerful, deeply personal prose. He makes his appeal through his own tragic/heroic story and through suggesting that a close look at this story will, if there's any justice, lead to methods of change.

Douglass's narrative is one of the most heroic and striking examples of romantic/pragmatic rhetoric in action as it embodies the self in its public discourse and its social agenda. But Margaret Fuller is not far behind Douglass in the drama of forging the complicated path that romantic/pragmatic rhetoricians followed when they attempted to make notions of self and other, individual and community, work together in theory and in practice. Fuller, in fact, resembles Douglass perhaps more closely than other romantic writers in America. She struggled resolutely against an enormous wall of resistance as she tried to live out the consequences of the romantic theories she had adopted. Although the differences between them are clear, including the fact that Douglass is a more gifted writer than Fuller, the similarities are notable. The burdens of sex and gender resemble in kind, if not in degree, those of slavery, and thus the struggle of these two American romantics becomes all the more heroic.

Margaret Fuller was the primary female American romanticist; a partner with Emerson in the editing of the transcendentalist magazine the *Dial*, the first American female journalist and foreign correspondent, the first critic, along with Edgar Allan Poe, of an emerging national literature, a feminist whose writings about the role of women remain radical 150 years after their publication. She was also a brilliant teacher and conversationalist, two qualities shared by many romantic/pragmatic rhetoricians and often as devalued then as now. Emerson thought her the "best conversationalist in America" (Blanchard 1987, 130). And her students were fiercely devoted to her, even when they didn't always understand her methods. One of her students wrote home from Bronson Alcott's school where Fuller taught for several months that "she [Margaret] said that it must not be our object to come and hear her talk. We might think it a delightful thing to her to talk to so many interesting auditors, but that was not the thing; she could not teach us so, *we* must talk and let her understand our minds" (121). Visionary words about teaching anticipating John Dewey and Paulo Freire were parallels to prophetic words about women and their status in society. Her "Conversations" were a series of professional discussions about changing the status of women, and these "lessons" augmented her income at the same time that they increased awareness of women's roles and the need for change. The Peabody sisters, Anna Barker, Sophia Ripley, Caroline Sturgis, and others, including at times Lidian Emerson, made up the core of this group. Men were excluded because Fuller's primary purpose in these talks was to alter the image women had of themselves. As her biographer Paula Blanchard puts it, "She wanted to help women overcome the double educational and social handicap by forcing them to fully engage their minds in an atmosphere that was as free as possible from censure" (147). Continuing for four years, the Conversations chose broad topics from Culture to Hygiene and prepared Fuller for the feminist work she was soon to accomplish in the *Dial* and in her book *Woman in the Nineteenth Century.*

In her essay in the *Dial*, "The Great Lawsuit. Man vs. Men: Woman vs. Women," Fuller challenges her American readers to consider the definition of liberty, linking the abolitionist cause to emancipation for women of all races:

> Knowing that there exists, in the world of men, a tone of feeling towards women as towards slaves, such as is expressed in the common phrase, "Tell that to women and children"; that the infinite soul can only work through them in already ascertained limits; that the prerogative of reason, man's highest portion, is allotted to them

in a much lower degree; that it is better for them to be engaged in active labor, which is to be furnished and directed by those better able to think, &c. &c. (1994, 530)

The essay is radical in its insistence on sexual liberation (its defense of the scandalous George Sand and Mary Wollstonecraft), on equality of opportunity in the workplace ("Such duties are inconsistent with those of a mother; and then we have ludicrous pictures of ladies in hysterics at the polls, and senate chambers filled with cradles" [531]), and in its recognition of power relationships that determine social and political laws ("But that is the very fault of marriage, and of the present relation between the sexes, that the woman does belong to the man, instead of forming a whole with him" [53]).

Like Douglass, Fuller uses her own experience, masked by the pseudonym Miranda, as a mirror of women's experience. A narrative of her education and her relationships with men and women, the story of Miranda becomes part of Fuller's larger contention about inequality and her exhortation for justice. The personal story as proof and method is a characteristic of much romantic writing, but not primarily because of the often-cited belief in the sanctity of the individual experience. It is proof precisely because it is not merely individual experience but personal life as it is experienced by many individuals, and Fuller's imperative tone, like Thoreau's, is not mere exhortation but illustration of the ways in which women might change their own lives and those of their sisters. Telling the story is one of those methods. Fuller's rhetoric and style partake of what Donna Dickerson, editor of *Woman in the Nineteenth Century*, calls "romantic feminism," as Fuller looks for liberation through psychological means and prefigures modern feminists with her assertion of "a different voice." Romanticism, Dickerson notes, fit the emerging feminist agenda: "Romanticism values diversity and assigns positive value to gender differences" (1994, xxviii). Although some, if not most, male romantic writers remained aggressively antifeminist, the ideal of romantic thought appears to offer hope for women in its assertions of the value of difference and of change.

Despite its sometimes tortured nineteenth-century prose, Fuller's essay is strikingly modern in many ways, a characteristic shared by many romantic/pragmatic rhetoricians. Emerson anticipates Freire and Vygotsky and, as West argues, even Marx (1989, 30); Thoreau anticipates protest movements; Douglass anticipates autobiography as manifesto; Fuller obviously prefigures modern and postmodern feminism. Yet, unlike other romantic writers in the nineteenth century, Fuller was excoriated by the press and sometimes even her friends for her "scandalous" actions as well as beliefs, and her "overly romantic" sensibilities. Hawthorne, who Caroline Ticknor reports was so worried about "the damn women scribblers" (1913, 142), wrote about her with a kind of mean-spiritedness after her tragic drowning: "There never was such a tragedy as her whole story; the sadder and sterner, because so much of the ridiculous was mixed up with it, and because she could bear anything better than to be ridiculous. It was such an awful joke," he goes on, "that she should have resolved, . . . to make herself the greatest, wisest, best woman of the age" (Blanchard 1987, 194). Hawthorne's condescending venom betrays his own lifelong difficulties with the "dark lady" who is both strong and intelligent. Fuller's romanticism and pragmatism, grounded in her strength and intelligence, were no doubt harder for others to bear because she was a woman.

The romantic/pragmatic rhetoricians of the nineteenth century make the whole notion of self and identity into a kind of process of understanding the other; a process of discovery of individual identity becomes, necessarily, a discovery of Whitman's democratic vistas as well, a recognition of and plan for achieving commonality and community possibility. Among the nineteenth-century romantic rhetoricians, there was great belief in possibilities. The century demanded it, especially with the explosion of technology that began and sped forward during the period.

Nature, Technology and Mediating Principles

> These railroads give us wings; they annihilate the toil and dust of pilgrimage; they spiritualize travel!
> —Clifford, in *The House of the Seven Gables*

One of the most pervasive stereotypes about romantic thought is its aversion to whatever opposes the natural—the technical, or even the artful. Since romanticism is supposed to glorify nature, it must see what deviates from the natural as a kind of fall, or a perversion of beauty and innocence. At the very least, romantic writers are seen to align themselves in direct opposition to the technical, averting their eyes from the mechanical or the industrial and instead turning inward toward the natural. But American romanticism itself was an attempt to reconcile impending technology with natural ideology. Even after the Puritans, when nature could no longer appear an obstacle or a threat to the growth of a culture, and even after Fenimore Cooper's warning in *The Prairie* of the loss that attends the destruction of the wild and pastoral, the American romantic's impulse was complicated by a sometimes unwilling attraction to the technical. For the North American, technological growth signaled progress, and progress meant the growth of American culture.

Part of the uniqueness of American romanticism stems in fact from its dialectical relationship between technology and nature. Technology was both feared and admired, a symbol of possibility and of loss. And the primary symbol of technology in the nineteenth century was the train. Landscape art during the period provides a vivid account of the dialectical stance that Americans took in order to view the incursion of technology into their lives. Thomas Cole, for example, perhaps the most exemplary artist of the Hudson River School and of early-nineteenth-century art in America itself, painted landscapes that revealed first the transformation of the forest into the pastoral and then the pastoral to "civilized" nature as the train wends its way through fields in the background. His paintings in 1830 and again in 1846 show the attempt to integrate the railroad into the calmly beautiful countryside, and the integration appears to happen without much struggle. Unlike Cooper's hero Natty Bumppo, as Leo Marx puts it, there is "little to suggest that Cole regretted transformation from wilderness to pastoral" (Marx and Danly 1988, 197). In "River in the Catskills" in 1843, the train in fact becomes a mediator between the wilderness of the hunter who stands in the foreground and the cultivated farmland that lies in the distance. The train reconciles one to the other, creating a new kind of unity of land and purpose. Among painters like Cole there was little conflict between progress and the pastoral because the terrain that surrounded the train and village appeared boundless.

In much of early nineteenth century art, railroad construction was idealized as the symbol of progress, a visible sign of American potential for economic growth. The train itself was a romantic idealization, or could be. Marx and Danly's book, *The Railroad in American*

Art, includes photographs taken during an "artist's excursion," where a train equipped with a photography studio carried artists and photographers to publicize train travel and make "scenery known to the public" (16). One photograph shows a train crossing a bridge suspended over Niagara Falls. The natural and technological sublime merge. By the middle of the century, however, the early optimism about the peaceful and noninvasive relationship of train to landscape had been tempered. The move westward made the train and the ideology of progress more explicit, more dominant, and more threatening. Alexander Gardner, a photographer who publicized the Western expansion, wrote in 1867:

> We found the workmen, with the regularity of machinery, dropping each rail in its place, spiking it down, and seizing another. Behind them, the locomotive, before the tie layers; beyond these the graders; and still further, in the mountain recesses, the engineers. It was civilization pressing forward—the Conquest of Nature moving toward the Pacific. (Quoted in Marx and Danly, 16)

As Marx points out, this new landscape depicted by photographers and painters in the mid-nineteenth century reverses the traditional European landscape painter's art. Instead of fallen columns and decaying towers, there are fallen trees and cleared land. The romance of the past seems uniquely American—with progress itself as potentially destructive to the natural world. While in Europe art gives way to Nature, in America Nature makes way for a power that is at once celebrated and bemoaned. The double vision of struggle, both proud and fearful, optimistic and nostalgic, is evident in much of the painting during this period where train meets field and field meets wilderness. Capt. Frederick Marryat, a popular English novelist of the period, traveled along the Erie Canal in 1847 and makes this difference in romantic vision between America and Europe explicit:

> Extremes meet: as I look down . . . upon the giants of the forest, which had for so many centuries reared their heads undisturbed, but now lay prostrate before civilization, the same feelings were conjured up in my mind as when I have, in my wanderings, surveyed such fragments of dismembered empires as the ruins of Carthage or of Rome. There the reign of Art was over and Nature had re-

sumed her sway—here Nature was deposed, and about to resign her throne to the usurper Art. (Quoted in Marx and Danly, 107)

Asher Durand's 1853 painting *Progress* foregrounds displacement of the Indian and the ruins of the wilderness that surround him. The Indian stands on the precipice with ruins of trees around him. On the right the wilderness gives way to the pastoral, with wagons and cattle indicating the progress of the economy. Far in the distance, a train crosses a viaduct to ships docked in a distant port. This inescapably nostalgic, if peaceful, vision was reviewed in the *Knickerbocker* as a purely American work. "It tells an American story out of American facts, portrayed with true American feeling, by a devoted and earnest student of Nature" (quoted in Marx and Danly, 95). The American feeling the reviewer celebrates expresses the conflicting and ambivalent view Americans held of technology. In this painting and others of the period, decline informs the very setting that purports to glorify progress.

The Indian, like the wilderness, yielded to progress. And like the vision of progress itself, the American's view of the Indian was ambivalent. From early colonial days when the Indian was viewed as a threat, or even an instrument of the devil, the Indian becomes by the middle of the century more of an impediment to progress than a danger, and sometimes even a nostalgic symbol of the wildness that was the land. De Tocqueville, as he did in so many cases, spoke with elegant foreshadowing in *Democracy in America* when he noted that "they [the Indians] seem to have been placed by Providence amid the riches of the New World only to enjoy them for a season; they were there merely to wait until others came" (1945, 29). Often equated with the natural world itself, the Indian typically stands at the edge of the paintings in this genre, surrounded by wilderness, watching the progress of civilization. However, the view of the Indian is not always so passive or pristine. The pediment on the U. S. Capitol Building, completed by Thomas Crawford in 1854, depicts a colonialist subduing an Indian warrior who is savagely attacking a woman. The pediment is entitled "The Advance of Civilization" (Marx and Danly 1988, 58).

The notion that progress, or the advance of civilization, was unstoppable and therefore not susceptible to change lay at the heart of the combined optimism and fear that American romantics felt so keenly when they witnessed what the culture termed "progress" in action in the towns and in the countryside of the developing nation. De Tocqueville points to this belief:

> The wilds become villages, and the villages towns. The American, the daily witness of such wonders, does not see anything astonishing in all this. This incredible destruction, this even more surprising growth, seems to him the usual progress of things in this world. He gets accustomed to it as the unalterable order of nature. (1945, 329)

As one journalist put it, "Progress is God" (Marx and Danly 1988, 58).

The railroad's effect on daily life was evident. And its usefulness as a symbol is made clear in the art and literature of the day. It had an effect as well on the culture of progress itself, the definitions put to progress and the methods used to achieve it. As Marx suggests, the railroad revolutionized the whole notion of system in the world of commerce. No technology did more than the railroad to "hasten the rationalization and bureaucratization of business" (187). Progress could be speeded up by efficient workers and efficient technology, and the railroad both embodied that speed and made use of it in its newly emerging centralized corporate management.

Marx argues that people understood the profound changes that were taking place in society; unlike de Tocqueville, Marx believes that there was conscious awareness. But, as in our own time perhaps, in nineteenth century America there existed what Marx calls a "conceptual void," an inability to give voice to or to name those changes: "To read in the literature and the public discourse of that critical era, is to become aware of an enormous conceptual void and a yearning to fill it—to find some way, if not to explain, at least to represent what was happening" (187). Without the power to name change (even the term *industrial revolution* was not born until late in the century), change and progress became inevitably linked. Marx says: "What once had been perceived as change had acquired the unmistakable character of continuous, linear, predictable *progress*. Like a railroad moving across a landscape, the course of events itself now could be thought of as advancing, liberating, improving, beneficent or in a word, progressive" (190).

Visual art mirrored the subjects of literary art. The American romantics, particularly Emerson, Thoreau, and Hawthorne, were obsessed with the relationship between the technological and the natural, between progress and loss. One way that they attempted to reconcile their ambivalence about technology and system was to make the technical appear to be a kind of natural activity; if not to show that the two were one, at least to *naturalize* the technical so that it served human, and humane, ends.

Emerson felt both fear and pleasure at thinking of how technology might advance the cause of human imagination and freedom. In *Nature,* he lists as one—in fact the first—of the final causes of the world "commodity" (1985, 4). Nature is valuable, Emerson suggests, for its *uses,* the ways a society might find to derive benefit from it. Both nature and technology proceed from the same source and thus, in Emerson's formulation, are not in fundamental conflict: "The useful arts are reproductions or new combinations by the wit of man, but of the same natural benefactors. He no longer waits for favoring gales, but by means of steam, he realizes the fable of Aeolus's bag, and carries the two and thirty winds in the boiler of his boat" (7). Whether the winds are harnessed in the boat or remain in the gales, they serve the same end of use.

When Emerson speaks of the train itself in *Nature,* his metaphor specifically links the natural and the technical: "To diminish friction, he paves the road with iron bars, and, mounting a coach with a shipload of men, animals, and merchandise behind him, he darts through the country, from town to town, like an eagle or a swallow through the air" (6–7). The train loses its association with the mundane and becomes airborne, allowing the passenger to fly. The progression in the sentence from iron bars to the eagle and swallow is a move that connects explicitly the man-made to the natural, and the sweeping quality of the move suggests the optimism that such a connection provoked for Emerson.

In 1844, a decade after *Nature,* Emerson reiterates the connection between fear and delight as he comments on the power of the train in "The Young American": "Railroad iron is a magician's rod, in its power to evoke the sleeping energies of the land and water" (364). The answer for Emerson remains not to renounce technology but to subordinate it to the imaginative and moral life. Technology becomes a way to uncover the pastoral and the natural.

If Emerson was known for an optimism about progress and the individual, Thoreau appeared to claim a more cynical view of the relationship between the two. The experiment at Walden Pond has been seen by generations as a repudiation of the world that as Wordsworth put it was increasingly "too much with us." Thoreau's world appears to be the embodiment of the romantic desire to recover the individual spirit by immersion in the natural world in a rejection of the world of commerce and society. Thoreau speaks fairly often of the destructive qualities of the train. In one place early in *Walden* he disparages the train as a mode of transportation:

> [B]ut though a crowd rushes to the depot and the conductor shouts "all aboard!" when the smoke is blown away and the vapor condensed it will be perceived that a few are riding, but the rest are run over, and it will be called, and will be "a melancholy accident." No doubt they can ride at last who shall have earned their fare that is, if they survive so long, but they will probably have lost their elasticity and desire to travel by that time. (1966, 61–62)

And, later, his famous line, "We do not ride upon the railroad; it rides upon us" (61–62), certainly shows that Thoreau is not enamored of the train, recognizing its dangers for the natural world, and its dangers for the possibility of community.

Yet his attraction to the train appears as well. The train circled the edge of Walden Pond and Thoreau could watch its smoke as he sat in front of the fire in the morning. He walked along the tracks to Concord to visit his mother, collect supplies, or to talk with Emerson. And he speaks fondly about what the train means to him in his experiment at Walden:

> The Fitchburg Railroad touches the pond about a hundred rods south of where I dwell. I usually go to the village along its causeway, and am, as it were, related to society by this link. The men on the freight trains, who go over the whole length of the road, bow to me as to an old acquaintance, they pass me so often, and apparently they take me for an employee; and so I am. I would fain be a track-repairer somewhere in the orbit of the earth. (190)

The metaphor Thoreau chooses is less overtly conciliatory than Emerson's, but it is mediating nonetheless. Thoreau links himself to the technical as he becomes a track-repairer of broken spirits, a fellow employee whose job is messenger of hope to the mass of men living in quiet desperation. As he was well aware, the train allowed the message to travel far. This recognition of the communicative possibilities of technology underlies the drama of the ice-cutting scene from *Walden*. Thoreau comments first on the workers, who arrived from Cambridge with tools and wagons to transport blocks of ice for customers across the world. The section begins with Thoreau's distress over the workers' destruction of the natural beauty of the frozen ponds but ends in a more satisfied tone as Thoreau envisions the message spread around the world to those thirsting for it: "Thus it appears that the sweltering inhabitants of Charleston and New Orleans, of Madras and Bombay and Calcutta, drink at my well" (196–97). Ideas move, connect, and are transformed in a process the train both speeds and nurtures.

It's the notion of spreading ideas and transformation of old doctrines that most intrigues the American romantics even when they view the train, as Thoreau did, with suspicion or even hostility. The attitude is perhaps most vividly demonstrated in Hawthorne's novel *The House of the Seven Gables*, a story that turns upon the relationship of past and future and the need to embrace the new to escape the tragic burdens of the old. For Clifford and Hepzibah, the two characters in the novel most burdened by the past, the train becomes a momentary savior, a literal as well as symbolic method of escape. Their wild train ride in the middle of the night after they have discovered Judge Pyncheon dead in his chair in the ancient house becomes the occasion for Clifford to comment on the symbolic significance: "This admirable invention of the railroad—with the vast and inevitable improvements to be looked for, both as to speed and convenience—is destined to do away with those stale ideas of home and fireside, and substitute something better" (1967, 260). Progress moves us forward, brushes away old ideas, allows us to find freedom. Clifford, of course, can't sustain the excitement. After his glowing comment that reprises Emerson's—"These railroads give us wings!"—he retreats to passive obedience, looking to poor Hepzibah for guidance and suddenly fearful of the great machine he has lauded moments before.

Technology and method itself could only be reconciled by making technology a means for finding a way back into the imaginative life. Clifford's sudden hope for transformation of the old, Thoreau's transmission of the life of Walden to places far removed from its circle, Emerson's spiritual re-energizing, are pragmatic ways the romantics had for making technology a means of abandoning stultifying ideas and promoting new ones. In their less optimistic moments, the romantics feared the loss of the natural world and the imposition of the technical, feared that in a contest the victor would always be the *progressive.* Emerson's cry "the machine unmans us," Thoreau's grim "a few are riding but the rest are run over," and Clifford's sudden reversion to near catatonia as the train stops, all sound clear enough warnings about the dangers of new method and technology.

Contemporary writers and teachers are no less caught in the grip of a tension between the natural and technical. At the very moment that the narrative is recovered in the ethnographic work of a host of teacher/researchers, the backlash to narrative comes in strident calls for "objective" assessment, for end-of-course standardized tests in the public schools, for replicable data and designs in composition programs. Recently, at Hepsie's university, faculty members complained that a job candidate's research, which connected personal narrative and case study analysis, was too difficult to judge objectively. "I wouldn't know how to evaluate this for promotion or tenure," one said, shrugging. "It's not a novel. And I don't know what it is." The candidate was not hired. Another unsuccessful job candidate at Kate's former university endured the same criticism; he was "too involved" with the subjects of his ethnographic research, too "close" to see objectively, and he "cared" about them too much. The diminishing of the personal story, the lived experience, the local context, continues, framed in terms that make the "technical" the scientific and the supportable, and the "natural" the mystical and illogical.

In an essay in *The Politics of Writing Instruction: Postsecondary,* Tom Newkirk attests to the continuing devaluing of the "natural" as he describes the way scholars have approached the continually growing popularity of the ethnographic study or case analysis as a part of composition research, noting that the case study is still regarded as more liable to the demons of "subjectivity" and "personality" than empirical research. Even among research studies like Lauer and Asher's *Composition Research* that appear to be sympathetic to qualitative research, Newkirk finds the tolerance linked to an understanding that qualitative research is preliminary to other, more stringent or "objective" research methods. "Lauer and Asher note eleven problems in interpreting naturalistic research, all having to do with problems of human interpretation and selection of data," Newkirk notes (1991, 127). Although ethnographic research seems more and more credible, the "conspiracy against experience," as Newkirk calls it, continues. As Stephen North points out in *The Making of Knowledge in Composition,* "lore and practitioner knowledge have been for most official purposes anyway effectively discredited. It is now a second class sort of knowledge, rapidly approaching the status of superstition—to be held or voiced only apologetically, with deference to the better new knowledges" (1987, 328). And as Linda Brodkey argues, "The academy has traditionally demonstrated a limited tolerance for lived experience, which it easily dismisses as 'anecdotes' or 'stories,' and in some quarters that intolerance is so great that any ethnographic narrative would be an affront to scholarly sensibilities" (1987b, 41). Few among the critics of naturalistic research have read the opening to *Walden,* it seems, where Thoreau reminds readers of the *I* breathing underneath all that writing.

FOUR

IMPERFECT THEORIES
The Pragmatic Question of Experience and Belief

> [We] learn to prefer imperfect theories and sentences, which contain glimpses of truth, to digested systems which have no one valuable suggestion.
>
> —Ralph Waldo Emerson, "Self-Reliance"

> Pragmatism unstiffens all our theories, limbers them up and sets each one at work.
>
> —William James, *Pragmatism*

Emerson prefers "imperfect theories" because they derive from the active mind, always questioning, leaning toward, searching for, seeing beyond. As he's aware, though, it's tempting to choose "digested systems," ideas already accepted and safe, if without "valuable suggestion." We must learn, he says, to prefer those ideas that are unfinished but whose very tentativeness give them the potential for truth and useful action. Learning is an action and a choice that people must cultivate and seek out. Emerson's own early realization that "men are convertible; they want awakening" became a central focus for his romantic/pragmatic rhetoric, grounded on the possibility of change (1960–82, 4:281). Emerson knew too that history and society lead people to lean toward predetermined structures, set systems, and traditional categories. In "Self-Reliance," he mourns the lack of willingness to experiment, to try on new theories, in a culture that can only see error rather than possibility. "People wish to be settled," he commented soon after this essay was published: "It is only as far as they are unsettled that there is any hope for them" (1960–82, 7:354).

Emerson's aim, then, is to unsettle, and thus to provoke change and hope. "I simply experiment," he says, "an endless seeker, with no past at my back" (7:360). Carlos Baker describes "Emerson the futurist" writing here, "but the past, and he knew it, was always there" (1986, 87–88). This chapter explores how romantic/pragmatic thinkers have grappled with the conflict between the desire to "remain settled" and the need for imperfection, how change must come from the choice to lean toward unsettling, imperfect possibilities, despite the weight of history, tradition, and system.

American Pragmatism's Imperfect Theory

The technological explosion at the end of the last century forced people to confront the conflict between scientific advances and a diminishing natural world. The American romantics viewed the technical and the natural simultaneously as potential combatants and possible collaborators in the enterprise of regenerating the spirit. But their talk of nature and technology remained dualistic; whether divided or in concert, natural and technical were separated into opposites, and the romantics spoke of them in either/or ways. One must give way to another, as in Emily Dickinson's bitter and funny poem on the imposition of the train on the pastoral landscape:

#585

I like to see it lap the Miles—
And lick the Valleys up—
And stop to feed itself at Tanks;
And then—prodigious step

Around a pile of Mountains—
And supercilious peer
In Shanties—by the sides of Roads—
And then a Quarry pare

To fit its Ribs
And crawl between
Complaining all the while
In horrid—hooting—stanza—
Then chase itself down Hill—

> And neigh like Boanerges—
> Then—punctual as a Star
> Stop—docile and omnipotent
> At its own stable door—

Like Emerson and Thoreau, Dickinson mistrusts the train, recognizing at once its power and its potential destructiveness. And her insight in this poem is the irony of attempting to make the technical force into something natural. No matter what it was called, Dickinson knew, the train was something far different from a horse of iron. Her suspicion of the technical, especially when it was marketed as natural, makes her shy away from it. Henry Adams, writing twenty or so years after Dickinson, shares that suspicion. But by the time he was writing the *Education*, a new theoretical approach being discussed among New England philosophers offered a method for going beyond mistrust, and locating ways to see relationship rather than simple opposition. This approach was defined and named by Charles Sanders Peirce as *pragmatism*, and Henry Adams's chapter from his 1900 autobiography, "The Dynamo and the Virgin," presents a vivid metaphor for understanding this new mediated relationship.

Adams had visited the Great Exposition at the World's Fair in Paris in 1900 and had seen there a giant dynamo, a miraculous technical achievement of the time. His French guide, however, seemed singularly unimpressed, describing it as merely an "ingenious channel for conveying somewhere the heat latent in a few tons of poor coal hidden in a dirty enginehouse" (1961, 380). The guide's description of the banality of the machine leads Adams, as he recounts it in the *Education*, to consider the relationship between art and the technical. Echoing Dickinson's sarcastic comparison of the train's sound as "stanza," Adams describes artists' perception of machines as powerful but uninspiring: "They felt a railway train as power; yet they and all other artists constantly complained that the power embodied in a railway train could not be embodied in art. All the steam engines in the world could not, like the Virgin, build Chartres" (388). But Adams himself had marveled over the dynamo and marveled over the Virgin as well, and the two together begin to provoke in him an awareness of connection as well as opposition:

> Here opened another totally new education, which promised to be
> by far the most hazardous of all. The knife-edge along which he

must crawl, like Sir Lancelot in the twelfth century, divided two kingdoms of force which had nothing in common but attraction: The force of the Virgin was still felt at Lourdes, and seemed to be as potent as X-rays; but in America neither Venus nor Virgin ever had value as force—at most as sentiment. No American had ever been truly afraid of either. (383)

How should the American view the power of art and nature when compared to the technical? In *The Pilot and the Passenger*, Leo Marx argues that Adams sees the technical in primarily ominous ways: "This bravura description, composed in the style of machine-age Gothic, evokes a premonitory shudder at the thought of what could be in store for those who tamper heedlessly with forces as absolute and supersensual, as seemingly anarchical, as electromagnetism and radioactivity" (1988, 180). It's in fact the fearful, all powerful element in technology that is part of what Marx calls the "lure of the retreat" evident in American writing. The technical in Marx's notion is not opposed to the retreat into nature but a part of it: "The idea of technology as the controlling agent of our destiny lends itself to such retreats from politics. To invest a disembodied entity like 'the machine' or 'technology' with the power to determine events is a useful way to justify disengagement from the public realm and a reversion to inaction and privacy" (207).

That kind of disengagement is precisely what Emerson worried over in his *Journal* as he considered the gap between his belief and his actions. And it worries Adams as well when he looks at the awe-inspiring dynamo and feels momentarily powerless. But Adams finds a way to escape the lure of the retreat into inaction by finding a way to mediate between art and science. In speculating about art/nature (which Adams links together in the symbolic figures of the Virgin and Venus) and its relationship to the technical (represented for him by the dynamo), Adams realizes that the American, attracted to the technical as progressive, is also deeply afraid of the natural and—especially—the sexual as uncontrolled. As he speculates about the role of the Virgin and Venus as female representatives of both art and nature, he finds the "knife edge" along which he must crawl. The connection between both art/nature and the technical is force, and the tension arises from questions about the use to which force is put. Adams begins to see the dynamo in its symbolic dimensions: "The dynamo began to acquire a moral force, much as the early Christians felt the Cross." Like the Cross itself, the dynamo becomes a "symbol of infinity" (1961, 380).

What Adams discovers here, in other words, is the principle of use that connects machine and art, and how that connection works. In fact, the American's fear of the force of art/nature can be blunted by seeing the symbolic "artistic" force of the machine: "Yet in mechanics, whatever mechanics might think, both energies acted as interchangeable forces on man" (384). To his surprise and delight (although that delight is always qualified with Adams's wry cynicism) he discovers that he does not need to renounce the machine to claim art nor to abandon the mystical in order to participate in the technological. This dialectic between dynamo and Virgin is interactive but in new triadic, rather than dualistic, ways, as Adams recognizes that both art and technology derive from the same impulse and provide the same function: they symbolize force and provoke imaginative energy. Most important is Adams's understanding that the force exists in the mind of the human responder; the interpreter creates the energy. Adams's recognition of a third factor that can mediate and bring into relationship separate or even opposed ideas illustrates the primary principle of pragmatism.

Adams is writing the *Education* twenty years after Peirce, James, and other leading New England intellectuals first described the principles of pragmatism at a meeting of the famous Metaphysical Club in 1867. The term came up when a member brought to the group a definition of belief as "something upon which one is prepared to act" (Kuklich 1977, 53). The clear link between action and belief in this statement and the discussion that followed led Peirce, in *How to Make Our Ideas Clear* (1872), and later James, in *Pragmatism* (1907), to establish philosophical principles of conduct that would require belief to be sustained through action and that would allow action to lead to belief. Peirce's definition of pragmatism, developed and refined throughout his work, is "Consider what effects, that might conceivably have practical bearings, we conceive the object of our conception to have. Then, our conception of these effects is the whole conception of the object" (1992, 124). For Peirce, pragmatism is a method of making ideas real by following their outcomes, by understanding how meaning connects to practical use. The effects of an object, Peirce argues, equal its conception. The pragmatic method—"what practical consequences might conceivably result by necessity from the truth of an intellectual conception"—explains how theories and practices work together.

The pragmatic method included, for Peirce, James, and their followers, these tenets:

- The most important subject of inquiry is human experience.
- Inquiry is a process of observation, hypothesizing, and experimenting.
- Human experience is always the test of conclusions.
- The more varied the sites of inquiry, and the greater the number of inquirers, the more useful the conclusions.
- An idea is defined by its consequences.
- Inquiry into underlying principles brings opposing ideas into relationship.
- This process of inquiry leads inquirers to contingent truths.

These tenets suggest that inquiry is both a communal and a contingent process, operating in local contexts and among groups as well as individuals, and its method is therefore necessarily collaborative, with action tested by many in a variety of circumstances. Collaboration, in turn, demands mediation among diverse experiences and perspectives. Further, faith in the process starts the inquiry and becomes its goal; inquiry confirms and transforms belief, so that as Dewey put it in his essay on Peirce written after Peirce's death, "habits of action come more and more to embody the real" (1924, 308). The motivation for this new kind of dialectic came directly from a deep need to reconcile an advancing scientific world with the world of belief, the same impulse that motivated Emerson, Thoreau, and Hawthorne, and the other romantics in the nineteenth century. In the first part of the twentieth century, Dewey demonstrated the same need in *A Common Faith*, his assertion of how faith and science might be compatible: "There is but one sure road of access to truth—the road of patient, cooperative inquiry, operating by means of observation, experimentation, recording, and controlled reflection" (1934, 32). In the late twentieth century, West and Freire express the same desire to mediate between the technical and the natural, and they use the pragmatist's agenda by calling for action (testable, assessable, sustainable) that can provoke and reinforce belief.

Dewey's words might describe West's and Freire's methods of inquiry: "The method of intelligence is open and public. The doctrinal method is limited and private" (39). Like the pragmatists Peirce, James, and Dewey, these current pragmatists share a belief in the benefits of inquiry for an eventual realization of the "real": "Faith in the continued disclosing of truth through cooperative human endeavor," as Dewey says, and a humility about the results (26). Results are to be discovered or created only in mutuality, in a cooperative spirit, as well as in faith. The understanding of truth as partial and contingent is a key part of the doctrine of pragmatism and a key ingredient to its dynamic, non-doctrinal method.

As Adams discovered when he looked at the dynamo as force and the Virgin/Venus as force, the principle of mediation—and thus reconciliation— is pragmatic, determined by function or the possibilities for use. The doctrine of use is crucial to an understanding of pragmatic principles. Yet the problem with the term "pragmatism," ironically, stems precisely from its link with use; that is, pragmatism is concerned with use but not *merely* use. When a person says "I am pragmatic," she often means "practical," rather than theoretical, even expedient rather than reflective. What's practical is what will work, and thus the stereotypical pragmatist cares primarily, or exclusively, about ends or consequences. Knowledge in this sense is simply linked to function and outcomes. But a romantic/pragmatic rhetorician sees consequence as a part of epistemology and philosophical inquiry.

William James defines the pragmatic method as "the attitude of looking away from first things, principles, 'categories,' supposed necessities; and of looking toward last things, fruits, consequences, facts" (1975, 32). This different way of looking, this "unsettled" attitude toward categories, systems, and history can, indeed, "unstiffen" received theory, especially about knowledge and ethics. As James shows, pragmatism as a philosophical approach to knowledge is deeply concerned with use and consequence. But it is more concerned with the relationship between belief and consequence, connections between habits of mind and habits of action. James defines the pragmatic question as "What difference would it practically make to anyone if this notion rather than that notion were true?" (28). And he goes on to explain that, for pragmatism, "true" means "something essentially bound up with the way in which one moment in our experience may lead us towards other moments which it will be worth while to have been led to. Primarily . . . the truth of a state of mind means this function of a *leading that is worthwhile*" (98). As Emerson would say, then, truth more likely lies in imperfect theories and experimental action than in digested systems.

Because it is concerned with consequence, use, and human action, the heart of pragmatism rests in experience, in tested conclusions, and in verifiable data. It is therefore scientific, or technical, in its approach to the possibility of knowledge and truth. Peirce was testing new formulas for logic, for meteorology, and for astronomy, as well as a host of other disciplines based on new empirical methods. James was formulating new ways of approaching philosophy and new methods for thinking of the mind in the act of making meaning; he was the first professor of psychology—the discipline he invented nearly single-handedly. The strong emphasis on experience as opposed to *a priori* assumptions led to a different relationship between theory and practice and an altered vision of the importance of the participant in the experience as meaning maker. Peirce and James were preoccupied, consequently, with method, with how experience is embodied, might be accounted for and used toward the end of understanding.

Still, the pragmatists did not believe in an absolute empiricism. Writing just a little more than a decade after Darwin's *Origin of Species* had altered the traditional view of science and nature forever, and just a few years after the Civil War had altered the world of agrarian and urban life permanently, the pragmatists wished to find a way to mediate between experience and belief; in the face of crumbling assumptions about nation and humanity, they believed in fact that reconciliation between the two was necessary and real. Cornel West's discussion of pragmatism characterizes the Metaphysical Club's agenda this way: "The first articulators of American pragmatism . . . were learned professionals principally interested in demystifying science and, a few, in modernizing religion" (1989, 42). They were also deeply invested in reconciling belief and doubt. James writes in *The Will to Believe* that "When as empiricists we give up the doctrine of objective certitude, we do not thereby give up the quest or hope of truth itself. We still pin our faith on its existence and still believe that we gain an ever better position towards it by systematically continuing to roll up experiences and think" (1912, 17). And Peirce, the great logician and developer of scientific method, mediates clearly between belief and experience: "Faith in the sense that one will adhere consistently to a given line of conduct, is highly necessary in affairs. But if it means that you are not going to be alert for indications that the moment has come to change your tactics, I think it is ruinous in practice" (1931–58, 8:251, 187). What Peirce posits here is a triadic conception of the way beliefs and actions connect: action based on belief continually tested by experience and in a spirit of readiness and perpetual inquiry. Freire's definition of praxis is very like this Peircean third. Faith in a fact, as Peirce and James believed, can help create the fact. Indeed, James's project in *The Will to Believe* was to demonstrate that even the most empirical, scientific "facts" contain interpretive, individual, passionate elements and are subject to change given changes in individuals and in contexts. Freire's current statements about belief and action represent this position poignantly: "Dreaming is not only a necessarily political act, it is an integral part of the historico-social manner of being a person. . . . There is no change without dream, as there is no dream without hope" (1994, 91). Yet, facts alter faith as well. Pragmatic philosophy brings this triadic process—each side tested and altered by the other and by a third principle of mediation—to bear on history, experience, self, and society. Thus, this triadic relationship makes the dialectic tension implicit in romanticism an explicit part of the method of pragmatism.

Pragmatists, then, believed in inquiry (the method for experience to be tested) and in belief (the quality that inspires inquiry and experience) and in the symbiotic relationship between the two, symbiotic because the relationship itself yields new insights or third principles. Pragmatic theory is restless, unsettled in its conclusions and methods. It is an imperfect theory that looks for its proofs everywhere and in everyone. "It matters not to an empiricist," says James, "from what quarter an hypothesis may come to him; he may have acquired it by fair means or by foul, passion may have whispered or accident suggested it; but if the total drift of thinking continues to confirm it, that is what he means by true" (1912, 17). The test of truth is in its continuing effectiveness, and experience is the continuing test of effectiveness: "Grant an idea to be true," pragmatism says, then ask "what concrete difference will its being true make in anyone's actual life" (1975, 97). This reciprocal relationship turns on belief, not in digested, immutable "Truth," but in the value of the *search* for truth, or for what is "more true."

This recognition of the connection between experience and belief meant that pragmatists could not accept the either/or notions of subjectivity and objectivity, or of the technical and the natural, that much of the debate between "romantic" and "rational" or "idealistic" and "empirical" ideologies turned on. John Dewey begins *Experience and Nature* by noting the complexity:

> Experience is a weasel word. Its slipperiness is evident in an inconsistency characteristic of many thinkers. On the one hand they eagerly claim an empirical method; they forswear the a priori and transcendent; they are sensitive to the charge that they employ data unwarranted by experience. On the other hand, they are given to deprecating the conception of experience; experience, it is said, is purely subjective, and whoever takes experience for his subject-matter is logically bound to land in the most secluded of idealisms. (1925, 7)

The "weasel word" *experience* is both subjective and objective, what James called a "double-barreled fact": "Truth *happens* to an idea. It *becomes* true, is *made* true by events" (1975, 97). Experience escapes the trap of either/or notions in the work of the pragmatists by becoming synonymous with "method." Pragmatic method keeps thinkers from having to choose between "rational" and "irrational" procedures, between what is logical, what is demonstrable, or what is desired. Pragmatic method insists that all of experience, not just what philosophers prefer to examine, be taken into account. Dewey explains the expansiveness, the "geniality" and "humility" of pragmatic method:

> When the varied constituents of the wide universe, the unfavorable, the precarious, uncertain, irrational, hateful, receive the same attention that is accorded the noble, honorable and true, then philosophy may conceivably dispense with the conception of experience. But till that day arrives, we need a cautionary and directive word, like experience, to remind us that the world which is lived, suffered and enjoyed as well as logically thought of, has the last word in all human inquiries and surmises. (1925, 11–12)

This attention to experience prefigures Freire's description of the process of praxis, where theories always come back to practices, where experience is the last word. Does it work? How? For whom? These questions make up Freire's definition of *praxis*—a process of problematizing experience and believing that such problematizing is worthwhile.

The lived-in world with its variety of experience and what James called the "blooming buzzing confusion" of sensation became one of the central features of the pragmatist agenda. As Peirce, James, Dewey, and their followers demonstrate, pragmatism's emphasis on real experience and its great variety insists that the agenda remain humble, never resting content with the truth of one's conclusions. New experience—which should come from any locale "no matter how unlikely"—can always alter theory and belief. In a dynamic universe, individual inquiries are never completely true. Therefore, pragmatic philosophy is constantly on the lookout for new experience to test past conclusions, including in that experience a reexamination of old experience, insisting that experience may come from anywhere and in any form, and acknowledging that the inquirer is always faced with the possibility not only of being wrong but the certainty of being not completely right.

This insistence on the limitation of individual knowledge complicates and enriches romantic ideas of individual value and individual perspective. The pragmatists demonstrated the limitations of individual knowledge, but they also asserted the importance of the individual as well. Although truth was partial and communal, pragmatism never forgets, as Dewey says, "the individual mind," which is "important because only the individual mind is the organ of modifications in traditions and institutions, the vehicle of experimental creation" (1984a, 20). Pragmatism illuminates the rhetorical character of romanticism by explaining how this mediation between individual limitation and individual possibility works. Dewey says that American "individualism" is "active": "The individual which American thought idealizes is not an individual *per se*, an individual fixed in isolation and set up for himself, but an individual who evolves and develops in a natural and human environment, an individual who can be educated" (20). In this same essay, written in 1925, Dewey characterizes the "current" individualism in America as "unreflective and brutal." But his belief in knowledge as action and consequence, and experience as varied and rich, give him the pragmatic faith, like Emerson's, in the "convertibility" of individuals and cultures.

The pragmatists' insistence that all forms of experience count also gave empirical sanction to the romantic emphasis on the experience of beauty and mystery by making it a part of inquiry, a source of possible knowledge. Dewey makes romantic notions of love, beauty, and belief overtly part of real experience and links them to testing: "we must conceive the world in terms which make it possible for devotion, piety, love, beauty, and mystery to be as real as anything else. But whether the loved and devotional objects have all the qualities which the lover and the devout worshipper attribute to them is a matter to be settled by evidence, and evidence is always extrinsic" (1987, 46) . This suggestion that devotion or love can be tested by extrinsic evidence links to the larger pragmatic agenda of making the whole variety of experience and beliefs, indeed, matters of testing and making experience and belief an intrinsic part of the empirical method.

This discussion should suggest that pragmatism, immersed as it is in practice, is not easy theory; it is neither ahistorical nor foolishly optimistic; it is not asocial or culturally naive, and it is not a plodding series of procedures. It is instead a set of philosophical practices that promotes a rational, experience-bound, communal basis for belief and a method for connecting individuals and the societies they operate within so that each might act on beliefs they come to hold. Cornel West continues to redefine pragmatism throughout *The American Evasion of Philosophy* as he analyzes the work of pragmatists during the nineteenth and twentieth centuries. Here is the definition he works out for the "indigenous mode" of pragmatic thought:

> Its common denominator consists in a future-oriented instrumentalism that tries to deploy thought as a weapon to enable more effective action. Its basic impulse is a plebeian radicalism that fuels an anti-patrician rebelliousness for the moral aim of enriching individuals and expanding democracy. (1989, 5)

West points to the pragmatist's emphasis on ethical and contingent dimensions of experience, as well as the impossibility, however seductive the attempt, to separate theory and practice. He cites Quine's definition: "Pragmatism could be characterized as the doctrine that all problems are at bottom problems of conduct, that all judgments are, implicitly, judgments of value, and that, as there can be ultimately no valid distinction of theoretical and practical, so there can be no final separation of questions of truth of any kind from questions of the justifiable ends of action" (quoted in ibid., 42). All problems center on action, all beliefs center on values, and truth and action come together in real ways only when the connections between them are made explicit.

Peirce wrote that "if there were an infinite community of inquirers and an infinite amount of time, inquiry would result in truth" (1958,
xx). The key word here is "infinite": Peirce was no essentialist, no
foundational thinker. He knew—and asserted—principles about limitation, context, doubt. The move here is toward movement itself, the
conviction that time, community, and system work toward the end of
truth. The belief in the possibility of coming to truth separates Peirce's
and West's pragmatism from later theorists called "neopragmatists."
As West says, "[O]f course such ultimate agreement never comes; it is
simply a regulative ideal and a hope that sustains rational adjudica-
tion and motivates scientific inquiry in the present" (1989, 51). Peirce
also does not mean that faith in possibilities should be blind or merely
hopeful; for Peirce, faith was always contingent and contextual:

> We cannot be quite sure that the community ever will settle down
> to an unalterable conclusion upon any given question. Even if they
> do so for the most part, we have no reason to think the unanimity
> will be quite complete, nor can we rationally presume any over-
> whelming consensus will be reached upon every question. All that
> we are entitled to assume is in the form of a hope that such conclu-
> sion may be substantially reached concerning the particular ques-
> tions with which our inquiries are busy. (1931–58, 5.384, 242–43)

This hope is a belief in the possibility of truth or, put another way,
reason to hope for possibility of change. Locating truth as a future
possibility—revisable, contingent, cumulative—allows Peirce and his
followers to avoid both determinism and relativism.

Until the last decade of the twentieth century, the most accessible
and useful collection of Peirce's essays was *Chance, Love and Logic*, a title
that represents the three tenets of his pragmatism: emphasis on contingency (chance), faith in possibility (love), and a systematic method
of inquiry (logic). Although Peirce is certainly the most central and
influential American pragmatist, his writing is nearly impenetrable,
the presentation of his ideas diffuse and, ironically, unsystematic. The
two American philosophers who followed, extended, and modified
Peirce's work made pragmatism more accessible, although neither is
primarily associated with pragmatic philosophy. William James, who

popularized pragmatism for his students and the American public, defined pragmatism in much the same way as Peirce had, but reinforced the doctrine of consequence:

> The ultimate test for us of what a truth means is indeed the conduct it dictates or inspires. But it inspires that conduct because it first foretells some particular turn to our experience which shall call for just that conduct from us. And I should prefer to express Peirce's principle by saying that the effective meaning of any philosophic proposition can always be brought down to some particular consequence, in our future practical experience, whether active or passive; the point lying rather in the fact that the experience must be particular, than in the fact that it must be active. (1978, 124)

The emphasis on concrete experience led James to assert, in matters of philosophical dispute, that "there can *be* no difference which doesn't *make* a difference" (125).

The emphasis on the particular doesn't negate the general; likewise, the assertion of the general is not merely connected to but dependent on the particular in Peirce's scheme. Still, Peirce was annoyed enough at what he thought of as James's co-opting the term that he replied testily to James's redefinition: "The writer, finding his bantling 'pragmatism' so promoted, feels that it is time to kiss his child good-bye and relinquish it to its higher destiny; while to serve the precise purpose of expressing the original definition, he begs to announce the birth of the word 'pragmaticism,' which is ugly enough to be safe from kidnappers" (1931–58, 5:402, 276). "Pragmaticism" might have been ugly enough, but Peirce was right to be worried about the ways his first term might be mishandled. As we've already shown, "pragmatism" has been used in many conflicting ways, even by its practitioners, and accused, by its detractors, of many faults, among them being both too "romantic" and too "practical."

Dewey's definition sounds quite similar to both Peirce's and James's: "Pragmatism, thus, presents itself as an extension of historical empiricism, but with this fundamental difference, that it does not insist upon antecedent phenomena but upon consequent phenomena; not upon the precedents but upon the possibilities of action. And this change in point of view is almost revolutionary in its consequences" (1984a, 12). Dewey, of course, was preeminently an educator, and his work on pragmatism connects more directly to current theory, pedagogy, and contexts than perhaps earlier pragmatists do. Like Paulo Freire, Dewey recognized teaching as deeply political. No less than capitalism and the struggle for control over the market, education is about power. As West puts it "[T]he struggle over knowledge and over the means of its disposal was a struggle about power, about the conditions under which cultural capital (skills, knowledge, values) was produced, distributed and consumed" (1989, 83).

West describes Dewey as "opening his eyes" onto the "social misery" that existed in the late nineteenth century: "economic deprivation, cultural dislocation, and personal disorientation" (80). Already committed to principles of an industrial democracy and excited by the reform movement in Chicago, particularly the work of his friend Jane Addams at Hull House, Dewey was further radicalized in the summer of 1894, finding himself on a train to his new job at the University of Chicago at the height of the Pullman strike. Reacting to a severe cut in wages by Pullman Car Works, and to Pullman's refusal to hear workers' grievances, Pullman's labor force went on strike on 11 May. With the support of Eugene Debs's American Railway Union, workers refused to work on any railroad with Pullman cars in its trains. So inspired was Dewey by the strikers' cause that he wrote to his wife, after talking to a union organizer at a stop along the way: "I felt as if I had better resign my job teaching and follow him around till I got into life" (JD to Alice Dewey, 2 July 1894, in *Dewey Papers,* quoted in Westbrook 1991, 87). After the strike collapsed less than a month later, with Debs arrested and federal troops guarding the railroads, Dewey was more than ever convinced that the class conflict he witnessed as he rode into Chicago was antithetical and dangerous to the democratic principles he loved. As a philosopher and academic, Dewey looked carefully around him and considered the consequences of what he saw: an exploding population with a larger and larger percentage in poverty; the rise of unrestrained big business, fed by an apparently inexhaustible supply of raw materials, including groups of people— the poor, immigrants, children—who represented to business the cheapest of labor, and a growing network of transportation. By Dewey's time, the train that inspired such hope and dread in the words of the nineteenth-century American romantics was no longer even remotely a pastoral symbol, and a retreat from its advances seemed less and less a possibility. The "industrial revolution," often taught unreflectively in the twentieth century as a thoroughgoing benefit to American culture, became the backdrop for Dewey's critique, and the impetus for Dewey's pragmatic project. West says Dewey's response to what he saw as a crisis in American culture took three forms: a foray into radical popular journalism, a humanitarian effort to introduce immigrants into the American mainstream, and a decision to influence the expanding teaching profession through his own teaching and writing (1989, 80). This third response forms the largest part of Dewey's legacy; he is remembered most as an educator, obviously. Yet, ironically, his memory is often associated with romantic, idealistic notions of education while his pragmatism remains forgotten. Dewey is, however, the last self-proclaimed American pragmatist to have any real impact on teaching. When Dewey names the new perspective that pragmatism offers as "revolutionary," he means it as a romantic/pragmatic rhetorician: "revolution" is not merely a word but also an action.

Dewey's vision was to create an "organized, articulate Public," made up of individuals in community, who could use, not be used by, the industrial age: "The highest and most difficult kind of inquiry and a subtle, delicate, vivid and responsive act of communication must take possession of the physical machinery of transmission and circulation and breathe life into it. When the machine age has thus perfected its machinery it will be a means of life and not its despotic master" (1984b, 184). Dewey was not nostalgic; he had what West calls a "no-turning back" attitude toward the "machine age" (1989, 106). His own progressive Laboratory School revolved around a core curriculum of "occupations"—activities such as carpentry, cooking, building, and farming that formed the "practical" basis for his theoretical assumptions that children need "opportunities for the evolution of problems out of immediate experience" (1976b, 135) and activity that connects meaningfully to the world outside the classroom. Dewey described his vision for American education in a letter to his wife shortly after he arrived at Chicago as head of the Philosophy Department:

> There is an image of a school growing up in my mind all the time; a school where some actual and literal constructive activity shall be the center and the source of the whole thing, and from which the work should be always growing out in two directions—one the social bearings of that constructive industry, the other the contact with nature which supplies it with its materials. I can see, theoretically, how the carpentry, etc. in building a model house shall be the cen-

ter of social training on the one side and the scientific on the other, all held within the grasp of a positive concrete physical habit of eye and mind. (JD to Alice Dewey, 1 November 1894, in *Dewey Papers,* quoted in Westbrook 1991, 96)

More than problem solving, then, Dewey wanted to teach American children how to be "alert" rather than "docile" (1976b, 135). Like Emerson, he believed that education should provide the "awakening" that human nature desires. At Chicago he convinced the Board of Trustees that pedagogy should be a separate department, and he wrote to Alice that "I sometimes think I will drop teaching philosophy directly, and teach it via *pedagogy.* When you think of the thousands and thousands of young ones who are practically ruined negatively if not positively in the Chicago schools every year, it is enough to make you go out and howl on the street corners like the Salvation Army" (JD to Alice Dewey, 1 November 1894, in *Dewey Papers,* quoted in Westbrook 1991, 95).

The Dewey School opened in Chicago in 1896. The school was Dewey's attempt to keep "theoretical work in touch with practice," as he also said in this letter. The school began with sixteen students, students who Dewey insisted were not "blank slates" but "already intensely active," with "native impulses . . . to communicate, to construct, to inquire, and to express in finer form" (1976c, 25–30). In language that sounds remarkably similar to Freire's definition of literacy as "reading the word and the world," Dewey insists that his school's subject matter was to be the embodied experience of the human race, including the experience of the pupils:

> The facts and truths that enter into the child's present experience, and those contained in the subject-matter of studies, are the initial and final terms of one reality. . . . To oppose one to the other is to oppose the infancy and maturity of the same growing life; it is to set the moving tendency and the final result of the same process over against each other; it is to hold that the nature and the destiny of the child are at war with each other. (1976a, 2:278)

Dewey wanted teachers to be highly skilled professionals, capable of helping students see the connections between school and community and reflect on how action is implicated in any act of knowing. This school was, indeed, engaged in "liberatory pedagogy": "Until the emphasis changes to the conditions which make it necessary for the child to take an active share in the personal building up of his own problems and to participate in methods of solving them (even at the expense of experimentation and error) mind is not really freed" (1980, 237). Dewey's emphasis on beginning where the students were lay at the heart of his democratic program. But he was not willing to leave them there. His ultimate goal was the creation of a "*community* of spirit and an end realized through *diversity* of powers and acts," a school "animated by a desire to discover in administration, selection of sub-ject-matter, methods of learning, teaching, and discipline, how a school could become a cooperative community while developing in individuals their own capacities and satisfying their own needs" (1981, 192). This sense of belief in individual and community applied to the teachers as well as the students; Dewey boasted that "association and exchange among teachers was our substitute for what is called supervision, critic teaching, and technical training" (1980, 235). At every level, then, the Dewey school and Dewey's pedagogical "creed" aimed to make schools agents of social reform rather than social reproduction.

West notes the pragmatic character of this educational experi-ment: "In sharp contrast to curriculum-centered conservatives and child-centered romantics, Dewey advocated an interactive model of functionalistic education that combined autonomy with intelligent and flexible guidance, relevance with rigor and wonder" (1989, 84). West notes, almost in an aside, that the "functionalistic" character of Dewey's pedagogy can easily be mistaken for a merely "functional" education, a program that might rest content in simply preparing students to take their places in the system. It's just as easy to confuse Dewey's emphasis on wonder and relevance with the merely romantic. In fact, Dewey has been continually criticized for the fuzzy or romantic liber-alism in his child-centered educational program. Robert Westbrook says in his biography of Dewey, however, that critics have "overlooked" Dewey's attacks on the advocates of "child-centered education for their failure to connect the interests and activities of the child to the subject matter of the curriculum" (1991, 99). Dewey's program was not ac-commodation to either side, nor a blending of opposites, but a radical new method—both romantic and pragmatic—for looking at teach-ing, learning, and knowledge:

Just as, upon the whole, it was the weakness of the "old education" that it made invidious comparisons between the immaturity of the child and the maturity of the adult, regarding the former as something to be got away from as soon as possible and as much as possible; so it is the danger of the "new education" that it regard the child's present powers and interests as something finally significant in themselves. . . . Interests in reality are but attitudes toward possible experiences; they are not achievements; their worth is in the leverage they afford, not in the accomplishment they represent. (1976a, 280)

Like the romantics, Dewey believes in the worth of individual experience and in the possibility for democratic action. Like the pragmatists, he insists on testing experience through a process of observation and negotiation. Dewey argues for this mediating method in all of his writing; however, Dewey's legacy continues to be misread as merely romantic, not pragmatic or rhetorical.

Westbrook comments that "it is difficult to read through descriptions and accounts of the Laboratory School and understand how Dewey came to be seen by critics as a proponent of 'aimless' progressive education" (1991, 104). However, like Peirce and James, Dewey's insistence on mediation, plurality, and contingency make his philosophy easy to misinterpret. And the propensity toward either/or ways of thinking makes it difficult to categorize an approach that devoutly rejects dualisms, thus making it susceptible to all kinds of misreading. In Dewey's case, the misreading includes a false notion of Dewey's effect on American schools. When the Laboratory School closed in 1904, shut down by university politics and competitive infighting over administrative authority, Dewey left Chicago for Columbia University, leaving, as Westbrook says, "others to interpret, apply, and usually distort Dewey's pedagogical ideas" (113). Although his critics often speak as if Dewey's curriculum overtook American education, the truth is that his program has never been systematically put into practice, pragmatically tested in public education. And although Janet Emig, in "The Tacit Tradition," names Dewey as a forerunner of contemporary research and practice in composition, saying that "Dewey is everywhere in our work" (1980, 12), the heart of his educational praxis—in romantic/pragmatic rhetoric—remains unexplored.

FIVE

A WAY OF SEEING IS ALSO
A WAY OF NOT SEEING
Whatever Happened to Romanticism and Pragmatism?

> I am convinced that the best of the American pragmatist
> tradition is the best America has to offer itself and the world.
> —Cornel West, *The American Evasion of Philosophy*

> The pragmatists, then, were by and large too tough an act
> to follow.
> —Robert Schwartz, "Whatever Happened to Pragmatism?"

Dewey's romantic/pragmatic work in education might seem, perhaps, "too tough an act to follow." As West points out, pragmatism has surfaced in times of cultural and social crisis. But because dualistic thinking dominates in theory and practice, pragmatism has always been vulnerable to the kinds of criticism leveled at Dewey, attacks simultaneously on its expedience and its romanticism. Today, West claims, pragmatism rises once again to the surface of what he calls North Atlantic intellectual life

> because its distinctive appeal in our postmodern moment is its
> unashamedly moral emphasis and its unequivocally ameliorative
> impulse. In this world-weary period of pervasive cynicisms, nihilisms,
> terrorisms, and possible extermination, there is a longing for norms
> and values that can make a difference, a yearning for principled resis-
> tance and struggle that can change our desperate plight. (1989, 4)

We would like to share West's hope that theory might look again to pragmatism for potential solutions to our culture's ills and that teachers might see the benefit in thinking romantically/pragmatically about the conflicting demands placed on them and their students. But pragmatism and romanticism remain largely misunderstood and ignored in their practical consequences, if not in theoretical treatises such as West's, and they continue to seem more like artifacts—pieces of thought probed only to decipher the work of thinkers long dead—rather than living ideas to learn from.

Robert Schwartz, in "Whatever Happened to Pragmatism?," puzzles over why pragmatism's lessons have not been learned in the 120 years since it was first articulated with such persuasive force: "How could so much work go on assuming as rock bottom the very dualisms the pragmatists had shown to be so fragile, if not untenable?" (1988, 41). Pragmatism's work may be just "too hard," he notes; as a philosophical method, it was "too tough an act to follow" (44–45). Its program was massive, its scope all-encompassing, its requirements daunting—including change in society and culture and continual vigilance and willingness to alter anything when it proved inadequate. Pragmatism's emphasis on the mutual implication of individual and societal relationships, as well as its insistence on concepts such as belief and spirit and possibility, made it seem both too optimistic and too difficult to implement as a program within the context of the industrial revolution and the rise of a capitalist market economy. Schwartz says that the pragmatists pursued "bigger game" than their positivist counterparts, functionalists (not philosophers) of all kinds who set up factories, schools, government programs:

> The philosopher's task was to critically evaluate and clarify what was going on and try to devise better ways to understand mind, to inculcate knowledge, to develop sensitivity to art, to promote social cohesion, and to organize our political and economic institutions. The job was not only to deconstruct the past, to show where settled habits of thought and conduct had gone astray, but to take an active role in *reconstructing* the future. Philosophy is reconstruction. Furthermore, these projects were not and could not be undertaken from some neutral philosophical standpoint outside these practices. They were to be pursued from within, guided by the experimental method. (45)

The pragmatists took as their subjects of study the mind, knowledge, emotion, and connections to social and political structures rather than productivity, distribution, immediate outcome. They were, very definitely, out to change the world, hopeful of the possibility of reconstructing both the past and the future; and the kind of questioning required to do that led to a messy, time-consuming investigation into bases and consequences that positivists, concerned with outcomes and products, found irrelevant and time wasting.

Perhaps this program was "too hard." But another, perhaps more crucial reason for pragmatism's marginalization in philosophy and education is an outdated but nonetheless persistent metaphor that continues to limit the way philosophy and education look at history. Since the end of the nineteenth century, one model of development, replacement, adaptation, and success has dominated not only science but also business, education, politics, and the humanities. The model centers on a notion of change and critique based in Darwinian evolutionary perspectives on transition and displacement. These include:

- Survival of the fittest: Those in the best, strongest position, those most adapted and adaptable continue and thrive; those less suitable or competitive drop off the evolutionary ladder.
- Increasing diversity: Evolutionary change is characterized as a movement upward, as a ladder, going higher, getting stronger, building up.
- Increasing complexity: Systems and parts become increasingly differentiated as time passes and the ladder reaches higher.
- Inevitability: Chronological time determines change as one stage necessarily replaces another.

This model assumes that complexity equals sophistication equals currency; that simplicity equals naiveté equals outdated ideas and methods. These assumptions have crossed over from evolutionary science to business, psychology, cognitive studies, education, anthropology, literary theory—in fact, to almost all areas of critical, philosophical endeavor. This model of evolutionary behavior, popularized by Herbert Spencer, relies on replacement as necessary and desirable, and on novelty as necessarily more complex, more "fit"—and therefore better.

Postmodern theories of whatever stripe, which have become such an integral part of thinking in education, follow this evolutionary path, embracing complexity and asserting it as theoretical principle. Anything "post" or "neo" is a better model because it's newer, and more sophisticated, a comment on what has gone before and thus a better reading of the present circumstance. Often this assertion of sophistication and complexity is mirrored in the semantic and syntactic structure of postmodern writing: neologisms, a "playfulness" with metaphor and punctuation, ironic digressions and interpolations accessible to fewer and fewer people. The specialization required to play in this discourse becomes continually more narrow and always asserts itself as new and unique. Spellmeyer says:

> Within premodern societies, the learned man was typically the master of information valued for its immunity to change; today, however, the value of most knowledge rapidly decays once the luster of its novelty has dimmed. For this reason, the power of the knowledge class lies in the production of *estrangement* rather than in the preservation of stability. (1996, 901)

This privileging of novelty and difference always put theories in competition, not conversation. If "postcolonialism" or "postfeminism" dominate the professional conversation in English or composition studies, it will be because they are the strongest, the best theories, the most fit to survive. After all, they were strong enough to displace New Criticism, which had itself overcome "romantic, appreciative" reading. The evolutionary model, so ingrained in current thinking and practice that we don't even see it as a model, celebrates increasing complexity and inevitable progress.

Composition as a discipline has embraced this linear, evolutionary, competitive model more fully and quickly perhaps than other disciplines. Within the last twenty-five years, besides exploring new practices, theorists have looked to their own history in order to describe and argue for the changes they see as inevitable results of more complex thinking and diverse environments. Chronicled by James Berlin, C. H. Knoblauch and Lil Brannon, and James Murphy, to name just a few, the history of composition and rhetoric has often been couched in the language of evolutionary replacement, battle for survival, and extinction. Whether these historians despise the past or admire it, they organize historical movements into discrete units, one unit inevitably replacing the other. Winterowd's indictment of romanticism's influence on current teaching practices is but one representative of this genre: Knoblauch and Brannon indict Aristotle; Halloran praises him; Murphy yearns for Quintilian; Kinneavy blames Bain and Campbell; Berlin accuses the eighteenth century of giving rise to the paradigm that dominates writing instruction today. These canonical treatments of the history of rhetoric neatly categorize past periods as artifacts and characterize past rhetoricians as successful mutations—adapted to changing environments—or as fossils.

The equating of evolution—change determined by strength and adaptability to environment—with progress is evident in composition's theoretical work and classroom practice as well. Despite the process movement in writing and newer methods of portfolio assessment, despite new emphasis on collaboration and the acknowledgment of personal and public connections, the dominant organization in composition classrooms remains the relentless assignment sequence of description, narration, exposition, and argumentation, or some cosmetic variation on this progression. Though the "modes of discourse" have been dismissed in theory, writing in school still moves from personal (narrative = simpler) to public (argument = more complex, sophisticated). And the second—public argument, research—is almost always valued more highly than the first. To write personal story is viewed as "romantic," and necessarily prior to the more sophisticated, public, and "pragmatic" task of persuasion or explanation. The ongoing debate over academic discourse and personal writing, recently rehashed in *College Composition and Communication*'s "dialogue" between Peter Elbow and David Bartholomae, assumes a hierarchy with academic writing as the pinnacle and personal story as the unfortunate precondition to the development of mature, sophisticated public prose.

The radical revolution toward "writing process" pedagogy itself, described early by Donald Murray as individual, messy, and circular, quickly hardened into a lockstep series of tasks as students, no matter what the context, drafted, revised, and edited on a regular schedule. That change showed clearly that even a system originally inspired by and designed along romantic ideals of self, imagination, and freedom can become an assembly line with no vision of the overall purpose or even the individual elements in sight. Even the most organic writing "workshops" have also become sites where the scientific virtues of repeatability creep in, and where the managers plan the tasks in order to ensure efficiency. Elbow and Belanoff's *Sharing and Responding* organizes group work by managing and prescribing writers' conversation:

"If someone says X, then you say Y," or, "Respond in this precise way at first; then move to this script; then move to this script." Even the most open designs for writing workshops, where students choose their own subjects and create their own agendas for writing, remain caught in a model of efficient production where the individual gives way to social and the messy becomes publishable.

Composition theory is even more susceptible than history or pedagogy to this evolutionary model. In the last ten years, composition has looked to cognitive, linguistic, expressive, and social theories of learning, meaning, and communication for solutions to the problem of how to help students write better. Yet as each theory is embraced it's as quickly rejected, and rejected so soundly that to call it up again risks the label of "old-fashioned" or retrograde. When Maxine Hairston announced a Kuhnian "paradigm shift" in composition in 1982, she heralded the process movement as a "revolution," with the "winds of change" overtaking the profession, leaving old notions of English and literature forever behind. In the last three decades, composition has often embraced visions of itself as revolutionary, cutting-edge, and above all, new. Insofar as it fuels change and energizes teachers, revolutionary sloganeering probably does a lot of good. Yet this kind of fascination with the new resists reflection; the harm lies in ignoring the consequences or the sources of new approaches.

Berthoff characterizes this tendency in composition as "pendulum-swinging":

> [A]n idea which one year is everywhere hailed and celebrated vanishes the next without a trace. In its place appears another which may or may not be consonant, may or may not be antithetical. The new idea is not introduced in the context of preceding discussion, perhaps because its time in the spotlight is limited. . . . (1991, 279)

Berthoff describes "adhocism" as endemic to academics in general, a kind of intellectual "fashion," but she also argues that composition is particularly susceptible to pendulum swings, usually viewed as advancements, because the two arcs of the pendulum are polar opposites, "manifestations of one and the same thing" (280). This "pendulum-swinging between positivist and mystical poles of a dyadic semiotics is likely to lead to vertigo, if not to brain rot, and in any case it is a distraction . . . from our mission, which should be to confront the problem of multiple illiteracies . . . " (281). Berthoff points to the need for mediation between the merely romantic and the merely practical, the need for a triadic principle to examine and follow out the consequences of the model a discipline adopts.

For our purposes, one of the more severe consequences of composition's continuing embrace of the evolutionary metaphor has been the neglect of the connection between North American romanticism, pragmatism, and rhetoric. The evolutionary metaphor has led composition historians to overlook or to misread American romanticism's influence on rhetoric, and to ignore the whole possibility of mediation between the romantic and the practical. Pat Bizzell and Bruce Herzberg, who include no romantic or pragmatic writers in their influential collection, *The Rhetorical Tradition: Readings from Classical Times to the Present,* state flatly that the central themes of romanticism are "fundamentally arhetorical" (1990, 665). James Berlin, in *Writing Instruction in Nineteenth-Century American Colleges,* devotes an entire chapter to praising Emerson's efforts to "create a 'romantic rhetoric'" (1984, 42). Acknowledging the stereotypical association of romantic with "anti-rhetorical," Berlin sees Emerson as "the best argument against this line of thought" and argues that his rhetoric combines an emphasis on the individual with social and democratic epistemology and action (42). Berlin says: "Emerson's rhetoric is first and foremost a system of thought designed to reconcile philosophical idealism with the demands of a democratic society. I am convinced that those who find in Emerson a rhetoric of self-expression are mistaken" (55). Yet, Berlin portrays Emerson as a lone figure in nineteenth-century rhetorical progress, a merely romantic voice that failed to affect American higher education. According to Berlin's history, romantic/democratic rhetoric's promise died, killed by a common sense practicality in education that was both conservative and elitist. In Berlin's evolutionary explanation, a new, more sophisticated, competitive, and complex ideal of science and technology replaced commonsense philosophy, just as common sense had left romantic rhetoric behind.

Given the metaphor of evolutionary displacement and growing complexity within which he operates, it's easy to see why Berlin, nostalgic though he is for Emerson and what he calls "liberal culture," can *only* be nostalgic, and why he must read the history of American rhetoric as a movement of inevitable progress, crushing the individual Emerson along the way. His very nostalgia betrays his reliance on the model of supersession, since nostalgia is always "merely" romantic, always incapable of challenging or connecting to present practice or to current theory because of its definitive "lost-ness." Berlin's belief that an evolutionary shift from emphasis on the individual, natural, and organic, to an emphasis on the social, scientific, and technological, means that he can only see the past as finished. He cannot look more closely and pragmatically in order to ask what difference it made to education that Emerson's romantic rhetoric "died," and what difference it might make now to see that rhetoric as still alive.

Berlin instead focuses on the movement that he says destroyed romantic concepts. At the turn of the century, American culture's fascination with industry, scientific method, and efficiency overshadowed romantic possibilities, and looking at this context also provides a partial answer to the question of what ever happened to pragmatism. In fact, one could view the whole "efficiency" movement in the early part of the twentieth century as a misapplication of romantic/pragmatic philosophy.

If Emerson, Thoreau, Hawthorne, and the romantics were ambivalent about the technical, the scientific, and the efficient, most Americans by the turn of the century were mesmerized, and began to look to industry for their models and methods, not only for business but also for the home and the school. The culture as a whole became enamored of the ideas and methods of "the efficiency expert." Raymond Callahan's *Education and the Cult of Efficiency* offers the most thorough account of the efficiency movement as it affected American schools from 1910–29 and its legacy in educational practice today. The efficiency movement began, not surprisingly, in the railroad industry, with hearings in front of the Interstate Commerce Commission in 1910. At that first hearing, the Northeast railroads petitioned the Commission for increased freight rates, citing demands for increased wages from railroad workers. Arguments were advanced on both sides, but the most persuasive came from merchants' association witnesses, who cited a new system, "scientific management," that would enable railroads to increase wages and reduce costs at the same time. From this moment, Callahan says, America was "dazzled" by a concept that represented national genius for mechanics at its best. From 1900–1930, education in particular was "taken over," according to Callahan, by the ideology of business, which in turn was in thrall to efficiency and scientific management (1962, 19).

Callahan explains the appeal of scientific management to a society enamored of technology, worried about conservation, inflation, and waste and determined to make more money. Business magnates such as Rockefeller and Carnegie were national heroes. The muckrakers had called Americans' attention to waste; the utilitarian and conservation movements responded with methods for saving energy, time, and fuel while producing an end product in the most efficient and timely manner. The president of the United States, Theodore Roosevelt, linked the conservation movement deliberately to the larger question of national efficiency: "The conservation of our national resources is only preliminary to the larger question of national efficiency" (quoted in Taylor 1947, 5).

As early as 1907, the call for efficiency had infiltrated the school system, particularly school administrations. Ideals of efficiency and productivity quickly spread from business through the press to the schools, where McGuffey readers taught that hard work led to success; success translated into material wealth. "Earning, not learning" became the watchwords for an educational system pressed by an economy-minded public for more return on their investment in schools. In *Classroom Management,* a textbook for teachers in training that went through thirty printings from 1907–27, William Bagley wrote that classroom management was really a "problem of economy: it seeks to determine in what manner the working unit of the school plant may be made to return the largest dividend upon the material investment of time, energy, and money" (1907, 2). For the next twenty years, the metaphor of the school classroom as business and the student as product would overtake discussions in principals' offices and at national conventions.

Indeed, this metaphor still infuses education today: the "back to basics" movement is designed to prepare students to take their places in a market economy more quickly and efficiently; proficiency tests are used to weed out the incompetent and promote those who are ready; recent outcomes-based assessment procedures are designed to provide efficient, uniform, and cost-effective ways to measure success and, not coincidentally, to maintain the American economy by providing workers whose skills are determined by their level of schooling, and whose level of schooling is too often determined by "efficient" testing. Freire's most famous metaphor of education—the bank—shows how closely tied education has always been to issues of profit and productivity. The teacher in Freire's analogy "deposits" facts or "knowledge" into an "empty" account (the student) and then demands a return on her "investment." Information, held by the teacher, is the currency used in this transaction, and the currency never really leaves the "bank" (the teacher) since at the end of the term or unit, she gets it back again. (See Freire 1970.) Within this model, efficiency characterizes the ideal transaction: "In banking education, an educator replaces self-expression with a 'deposit' that the student is expected to 'capital-ize.' The more efficiently he does this, the better educated he is con-sidered" (1985, 21).

The connection between business and education was strength-ened by the "father" of the efficiency movement, Frederick Taylor, as he boasted that his system of "scientific management," originally de-signed to increase productivity within business by getting more, and more quickly, from workers, could be applied to all institutions. Taylor's system of scientific management was based on a detailed painstaking observation and on an elitist, classist notion of the potential intelli-gence of workers and managers. Taylor argued that most businesses and factories were inefficient for two reasons: faulty management and "soldiering" by workers. Workers did the least amount of work they could, or soldiered, he maintained, because they did not understand the overall organization of the business, they did not get the "big pic-ture," and they either were "naturally" inefficient because of innate laziness, or "systematically" inefficient, deliberately slowing down the pace of work. The methods of working (hauling pig iron or assem-bling parts) were handed down from worker to worker; this "lore" was inefficient, according to Taylor, who believed that there was always one best method for doing anything, a method that could be discov-ered through research. Workers would never discover this method on their own because, even with incentives, freedom, and responsibility, workers were, by nature and by culture, incapable of understanding the scientific basis underlying particular tasks. (See Taylor 1947.)

Taylor introduced a four-step system of discovering and imple-menting the most efficient methods for any job. This system, really a breaking down into parts and establishing a hierarchy where man-agement controlled in every detail the workers' tasks, began with time and motion studies for each task, followed by revision of the "task idea," according to the scientific principles that the stopwatch dic-tated. Each worker received an instruction card, which described in minute detail "not only what is to be done, but how it is to be done and the exact time allowed for doing it" (1919, 39). The "task ideas" were worked out by the planning department, consisting of the managers and the efficiency experts. Workers were rarely consulted; Taylor believed that "one type of man is needed to plan ahead and an entirely different type to execute the work" (37–38). He did, however, believe in "functional foremanship," his concept for teaching workers how to carry out their tasks. "Human nature is such that many of the workmen, if left to themselves, would pay little attention to their written instructions" (1947, 123). There were bonuses for workers who adapted to this system, but those who didn't were fired. Taylor's system was extremely specialized, with little connection to the overall goals or end products of the business or factory, at least for the workers. The system was practical and useful, allowing for prosperity and productivity. On the other hand, its view that the world had shifted— "In the past the man has been first; in the future the system must be first" (7)—was coercive and fanatical in its belief that systems are solutions.

Taylor didn't stop with factories. Believing that the country was suffering a "great loss through inefficiency in almost all of our daily acts," Taylor tried to convince his readers that "the fundamental principles of scientific management are applicable to all kinds of human activities" (7). Taylor's model of "efficiency" swept across America in the first part of the twentieth century. Popular magazines took up the theme, suggesting that efficiency methods apply to the home, child rearing, and of course, the schools. During these years, educational journals and conferences resounded with calls for scientific management of curriculum, teacher training, and the ways in which school days (and hours and minutes) were spent. Keynote speeches at the annual convention of the National Education Association, the meetings of school superintendents, national journals, and trade books were dominated by warnings and advice about how to turn the nation's schools into more efficient "plants" and how to reduce the "unit costs" of educating students.

Two examples from schools, past and present, can represent this national passion for efficiency. Frank Spaulding, superintendent of schools in Newton, Massachusetts, and later head of the Department of Education at Yale, spoke to the NEA convention of principals in 1913 on why scientific management must be adopted. He dismissed the argument that the "products" of education cannot be measured and went on to catalog what could be measured in terms of school's productivity: namely, the "unit costs" of instruction. Spaulding defined a "unit" as one pupil recitation, and argued that a "penetrating analysis" of unit costs could both reduce expenditure and improve the quality of the unit. Spaulding described the "value" he assigned to the units:

> I know nothing about the absolute value of a recitation in Greek as compared with a recitation in French or in English. I am convinced, however, that by very concrete considerations, that we ought to purchase no more Greek instruction at the rate of 5.9 pupil recitations for a dollar. The price must go down, or we shall invest in something else. (National Education Association 1913, 247–48)

Spaulding's solutions to the crisis of inefficiency, as might be expected, were to increase the number of recitations per week per instructor and to increase the number of pupils per recitation class. Callahan describes this kind of scientific management mind-set as the beginning of the legacy that schools and universities live with today. In what he calls an "American tragedy," Callahan argues, finally, that these "unfortunate patterns" have persisted in education from the turn of the century well into the 1960s and beyond (1962, 244).

If this seems an extreme claim, here's a current example from the management of a university. Kate has been a member of both a college and a departmental executive committee. As part of that assignment, she spent a good portion of each spring semester reading annual merit review files from her colleagues and ranking each person with a number from 1 to 5 (including decimal points rounded to the nearest tenth). She rated them in three categories: their teaching, their research, their service. How did the committee arrive at each number? For teaching, they looked at the numerical summaries of students' evaluations of courses and teachers, which, of course, also included numbers from 1 to 5 (rounded to the nearest one-hundredth). In response to questions like "this was an excellent course/teacher" and "this teacher motivates me to do my best work," students could assign a number between 1 and 5, and they wrote comments in response to open-ended questions like "How effective was this course, this teacher, your work?" At its weekly meetings, the committee debated whether to pay attention to the students' comments or whether simply to "go by the numbers." They also talked about what *counts* as service, how much *time* was spent on reading manuscripts for presses or how *often* a particular committee met, how much *energy* administering a certain program took. Finally, they *counted* pages of publications, *measured* an academic journal's or a press's relative worth, and evaluated each colleague's progress and *speed* in publication. The committee measured all this data with other, equally as certain knowledge about each faculty member's nature, spirit, reputation, *ethos*. Yet this knowledge was subordinated to the data provided; these committees were engaged in time and motion studies.

This committee believed itself engaged in the same kind of close observation and contextual research that Taylor's system advocated. But like so many of the applications of Taylor's system, what this committee does is to take their colleague's work out of context as much as possible in the name of objectivity, fairness, and efficiency. The implication of the review is also that there is one model of the successful academic life, just as Frank and Lillian Gilbreth extended Taylor's system toward finding and enforcing the One Best Way to Do Work (1924, 154). As in other places that embraced Taylor's system, the profit motive is the primary incentive, since better numbers translate into higher salaries. Of course the committee doesn't want to be merely romantic, or merely hopeful about a colleague's teaching and research and usefulness, but it errs, as a result, on the side of mere practicality. Because either/or thinking suggests that the only alternative to romantic hopefulness is numerical validity, and because the evolutionary model dominates, pragmatic/romantic rhetoric's mediating influence is ignored. Mike Rose says that educators, when in doubt, "count" (1985, 344). And the impulse to count, divide, measure and tally up is natural, especially in a discipline as unwieldy as teaching, especially the teaching of literature, writing, and literacy. That's why the impulse needs to be named, monitored, and challenged.

We have returned to the bean counters of the efficiency movement within this discussion of romantic/pragmatic rhetoric in order to show how that legacy of counting has remained with us, taking on new guises in the names of "progress," "objectivity," "assessment," "Total Quality Management," or in excited hopes and promises for computerized classrooms, the Internet, and the World Wide Web. In current contexts for teaching, whether the high school classroom or the university seminar, the scientific management model for teachers'/ scholars' work still informs practice and professional discourse.

Taylorism in its many forms has seldom been successfully resisted. Martha Banta comments on science's refusal to consider what James called the "wild facts" of experience, "uncouth forms" that did not fit neatly into new systems of management.

> Once science found itself descending into the realm of the human element, one would think its practitioners would realize the impor-tance of going beyond the divine abstraction of numbers toward the unholy mess James describes with glee as the "menagerie and the madhouse, the nursery, the prison, and the hospital." This is not necessarily the case. Rather than readjusting the idea of applied science and the social sciences to accommodate the presence of the wilder facts, "uncouth forms" were expected to do the adjusting: this includes all nature of men, but especially women, children, blacks, and immigrants—those social elements designated as the irrational forces requiring careful containment. (1993, 28)

Banta describes Emerson and James as "rarities" because they in-sisted that any system must account for what's not susceptible to ratio-nal control (29). These uncouth forms, this wildness, are always asso-ciated with the romantic, always in danger of being contained and managed by practical men who deny their presence.

Dewey, too, was well aware of the seductive appeal of "scientific" methods that seemed to offer rational solutions to diffuse problems and appeared to give validity and sophistication to education, a field often accused of fuzzy or irrational thinking. Writing in 1929, he warned educators of the dangers of being mesmerized by a false sense of "sci-ence": "It is very easy for science to be regarded as a guarantee that goes along with the sale of goods rather than as a light to the eyes and a lamp to the feet. It is prized for its prestige value rather than as an organ of personal illumination and liberation" (1984c, 7). To embrace "science" or "research" without understanding its grounding in close observation and experimentation, Dewey warned, leads to "a segre-gation of research which renders it futile" and to educators who "go at educational affairs without a sufficient grounding in non-educa-tional disciplines that must be drawn upon, and hence [they] exag-gerate minor points in an absurdly one-sided way" (50). Callahan notes the irony of John Dewey's being described in educational history as the advocate of practicality and utility when in reality he was one of the most vocal critics of the scientific management craze. Indeed, Callahan says that Dewey "stood almost alone in opposing the watering down of the curriculum," and he notes that "there were other more powerful forces at work than 'progressive education' in undermining the intellectual atmosphere of American schools" (1962, 263). Dewey understood the pull of the new, the latest, in a culture swept up in evolutionary metaphors. In a speech to the NEA, Dewey explained methods of change in school systems at the turn of the century:

> Consider the way in which a new study is introduced into the curriculum. Someone feels that the school system of his (or quite frequently nowadays her) town is falling behind the times. There are rumors of great progress in education being made elsewhere. Something new and important has been introduced; education is being revolutionized by it; the school superintendent, or members of the board of education, become somewhat uneasy; the matter is taken up by individuals and clubs; pressure is brought to bear on the managers of the school system; letters are written to the newspapers; the editor himself is appealed to use his great power to advance the cause of progress; editorials appear; finally the school board ordains that on and after a certain date the particular new branch—be it nature study, industrial drawing, cooking, manual training, or whatever—shall be taught in public schools. The victory is won, and everybody—unless it be some already overburdened and distracted teacher—congratulates everybody that such advanced steps have been taken. (National Education Association 1901:334–35)

Dewey saw how such changes, aimed at making education more scientific and learning more efficient, were hardly changes at all, but merely the "same old education masquerading in the terminology of science." The changes, he argued, made no difference "except for advertising purposes" (1907, 90). If it looks as if it's more sophisticated, more complex, more "fit," education can embrace it and congratulate itself on its own advancement. Thus, what Berthoff calls "adhocism" or "pendulum-swinging" in English studies can also be seen as a kind of public relations tool, a groping for complexity, sophistication, or novelty in order to look more evolved.

Richard Rorty, in *Objectivity, Relativism, and Truth*, accuses the pragmatists of pendulum-swinging: "American pragmatism has, in the course of a hundred years, swung back and forth" between scientistic and idealistic stances (1991, 63). Peirce, James, and Dewey, he says, "tried to break down the influence of old moral codes and replace them with an 'experimental' attitude in order to promote new forms of social, artistic, and personal freedom." And, they believed in truth beyond the immediate sensation; they were "holists," as Rorty describes them, who knew that meaning had no direct correspondence to reality (63). Rorty argues, like a good pragmatist, that the mediating force between science and belief lies in community, not in confusing notions about objectivity and subjectivity. In *Contingency, Irony, and Solidarity,* Rorty says that we should hope for a "poeticized" culture rather than hope that culture can be "scientized." He argues against faith, saying that "we can keep the idea of morality just insofar as we can cease to think of morality as the voice of the divine part of ourselves and instead think of it as the voice of ourselves as members of a community" (1989, 59).

Although Rorty characterizes himself as a pragmatist, he shows in this sentence how different his own "neo"-pragmatism is from the mediating pragmatism of Pierce, James, and Dewey. As Rorty himself allows, the pragmatists never denied the possibility of truth beyond the immediate community, and never insisted that people lose the voice of the "divine part of ourselves." Rorty's emphasis on community differs from Peirce's, for it resists speculating beyond the immediate and because it resides in language rather than in action. John Patrick Diggins makes language the differentiating factor between pragmatism and neopragmatism: "With the linguistic turn in modern thought, philosophy no longer has as its task the clarification of truth, morality, and virtue. Instead, philosophy is to be conceived as a language activity. . . . Whether the point of traditional philosophy was to interpret the world or to change it, the point of 'post-philosophy' is to find ways of legitimating what we say instead of proving what we know" (11). Unlike the neopragmatic question, "What can we say?," the pragmatic question—"What difference does it make?"—has always been both a practical and a moral one. The pragmatic question is both scientific and idealistic, simultaneously immediate and long term— just as discussions of merit pay, class sizes, and teaching loads are more than practical questions and require more than talk.

A discussion of their practical, moral and ethical consequences, however, is hampered by the model of "digested systems," the impulse to see intellectual history and pedagogical practice as an evolutionary movement toward more diversity, complexity, and multiplicity. As we have shown, the "standard" views of composition as a discipline adopt this view, dividing the field into competing camps, with clear winners and losers, and privileging current stances for their sophistication. What difference would it make if we looked at this history and this legacy from a different perspective? What if we tried on a metaphor that countered the evolutionary and efficient ones of commerce, competition, and progress? The evolutionary model, so dominant that it's transparent, is based in biology, in observation of the natural world, which is one reason why it seems so "natural," so intrinsically an explanation for all systems. Stephen J. Gould tells another story about how nature operates that might provide an equally natural explanation, but also a more profoundly and pragmatically useful metaphor in his book, *Wonderful Life*, an account of the rediscovery of the Burgess Shale.

Gould's story is an argument for the importance of looking closely, and looking again, without the blinders of digested systems. The Burgess Shale, first discovered in British Columbia in 1909 by Charles Walcott, contain the oldest fossils on earth, fossils of fauna so amazing, so diverse, and so divergent from any modern forms (or their known ancestors) that traditional scientific explanations of evolutionary development simply could not account for them. After their initial discovery, Walcott and the scientists who succeeded him in studying these astoundingly unusual forms first tried to place them in existing categories—crustacean, Precambrian—to explain away the anomalies they saw in a host of ways. When that didn't work, they ignored them, hid them away, forgot about them because they simply didn't conform either to current taxonomies or to prevailing evolutionary theory. These scientists could not see what they were looking at in the Burgess fauna because they did not have the language to name them, nor a model that could contain them. Gould describes Walcott as "America's greatest paleontologist and scientific administrator" [of the Smithsonian], but also as a scientist who "proceeded to misinterpret these fossils in a comprehensive and thoroughly consistent manner arising directly from his conventional view of life: In short, he shoehorned every last Burgess animal into a modern group, viewing the fauna collectively as a set of primitive or ancestral version of later, improved forms" (1989, 24). So predetermined were these first researchers by the dominant evolutionary model and so fearful of what another model might suggest—wildness in the universe, chance as a factor in change—that they literally could not envision any different way to look at the Burgess fossils.

The fossils were rediscovered on dusty shelves in the Smithsonian fifty years later. Professor Harry Whittington's reexamination of the fossils led him to conclude that they were "uniquely specialized," not "primitively simple" (176). In fact, the Burgess organisms do not belong to any known groups—they are new life—and in number and diversity exceed the entire range of invertebrate life known today. Gould describes Whittington as "weaning himself" from traditional views of evolution and taxonomy, culminating in a series of monographs on the Burgess Shale beginning in 1971 that show "the history of life . . . is not the conventional tale of increasing excellence, complexity, and diversity" (25). In *Wonderful Life*, Gould tells the story of the Shale research as a drama extending over seventy-five years, starring "the world's most important fossils, in part because they have already altered our view of life" (52). The villains, then, are hidebound scientists, caught in the trap of digested systems.

The Burgess Shale creatures met all the Darwinian criteria for evolutionary success: they were fit, they competed well, they adapted to their environment, and they thrived. But they did not survive; they are not the ancestors to any known living forms. They did not get more diverse or complex or highly evolved. They simply disappeared. The Burgess Shale's inhabitants challenge the prevailing assumption that change is predictable and inevitable by proving that change may happen in irrational and unpredictable ways, that chance may be more important to evolution than natural selection. But as the story of the Shale shows, it's an understanding that scientists and historians have been slow to accept. For fifty years science ignored the Shale because it couldn't see the possibility of chance in the evolutionary scheme, and when scientists did recognize that possibility, they couldn't admit it, because the whole idea of chance appeared to make the operations of the universe chaotic.

The great lesson of the Burgess Shale lies in its revelation of the dominant, Darwinian evolutionary model *as* a model, not a natural, inevitable truth about the way the universe works. The old metaphors of "ladder of abstraction" and "cone of diversity," both of which describe evolutionary movements from simple to complex and from uniform to diverse, cannot realistically describe the history of life forms—or of ideas. Tenets of Darwinian evolution that have been applied to so many systems—increasing abstraction, increasing diversity, increasing adaptability, inevitability, necessity, progress—can now be examined as contingent possibilities, not realities.

Yet, systems resist contingency. Gould says: "The false equation of evolution with progress records a sociocultural bias, not a biological conclusion, and one hardly needs great insight to locate the primary source of this bias in our human desire to view ourselves as the apex of life's history, ruling the earth by right and biological necessity" (1995, 44). This bias, he shows, suppresses "diversification and stability, the two principal themes of natural history," and chooses instead to see only a march of progress (52). Gould argues, like the pragmatists, that contingency represents the essence of history and its movement. And like the pragmatists, Gould argues the importance of seeing contingency as mediating rather than as the polar opposite to determinism or necessity. Gould has this to say about contingency as a mediator to the dominant model of either/or thinking:

> Rejection of ladder and cone does not throw us into the arms of a supposed opposite—pure chance in the sense of coin-tossing or of God playing dice. Just as the ladder and cone are limiting iconographies for life's history, so too does the very idea of dichotomy grievously restrict our thinking. (50)

In other words, it does not follow that an acceptance of chance, contingency, and "decimation," Gould's term for the randomness that forced the disappearance of the Burgess Shale's creatures, means an acceptance of despair and chaos. Gerda Lerner's essay in her recent book *Why History Matters,* called "Nonviolent Resistance: The History of an Idea," tells a different kind of evolutionary story, where an idea— in this case, passive resistance to oppression—does not follow the Spencerian model of growth, diversity, complexity, and replacement. Its story follows a new evolutionary path, more like Gould's analysis of the Shale.

Lerner begins with an account of Quakers' use of nonviolent resistance to the persecution they suffered at the hands of their Puritan neighbors during the first years of the Massachusetts Bay Colony, including Quaker Mary Dyer, who refused to accept banishment from

Boston and returned to the colony to be hanged there in 1660. From those early moments, the method of passive resistance to wrong grew in a number of directions, including the antislavery movement. Its dictum was expressed by Quaker John Woolman, who traveled across the South in the mid-eighteenth century witnessing against slavery and war. "Conduct is more convincing than language," he said, fusing action and belief. The idea of resistance and change through nonviolent action grew throughout the nineteenth and twentieth centuries, and found one of its most profound expressions in the work of Martin Luther King in the middle of this century.

However, Lerner's point in this small history of an idea is not that the concept of peaceful resistance simply grew better, bigger, and more complex as time passed and the characters changed. Instead, she challenges that view, noting that many before Henry David Thoreau had refused to pay taxes to support war or slavery, and that his act had little practical significance or heroism. It was his record of the act, the essay *On Civil Disobedience,* that made Thoreau's small act so monumental, as he "fashioned out of the common experience of his time and out of his deepest personal convictions," as Lerner puts it, a deep philosophical statement and an artistic creation of lasting resonance. "The idea depended for its spread and impact on the interaction of theory and practice," Lerner asserts (1997, 67), and that interaction made it both real and transferable. But those lessons were all but forgotten in the period of Reconstruction, when Thoreau's essay seemed, as Lerner puts it, "outdated and irrelevant. We see here one of those examples of discontinuity in history, when ideas which agitated and stirred one generation seemingly sink without a trace" (67).

Of course the idea did not sink. Tolstoy and Gandhi and King used it to agitate and stir other generations in other places in the world. But the theory they used and the actions they performed were no longer Thoreau's or the ideas of the Quakers. As Lerner says of Gandhi's work, "It was now a changed theory" (72). And it led to different actions and consequences, as the machinery of government itself stopped in India. The Montgomery, Alabama, bus boycott made new theory again, as the various strands of the idea of nonviolent resistance came together in new action.

Lerner's account points to the way ideas may get lost, remade, challenged, and transformed in a "discontinuous" process that is both unpredictable and unsystematic. They may die in one place and be reborn in another. In all cases, ideas are remade according to need. As Lerner says of King, he "reached for the appropriate theory when his practice demanded it" (73). And his actions, of course, generated new practice, new thought, and new theory to be used in later civil rights actions, initiatives for women, and the world peace movement.

Evolution, whether of a species or of an idea, can be full of surprises, it seems. For Lerner and for Gould, the possibility of surprise—and of the reorientation in thinking it requires—doesn't occasion regret or fear. As their work shows, historians, scientists—and teachers—need to know the living past, need to learn how to use it, and need to understand that circumstance and context alter ideas. Yet perhaps it's the unsteadiness of this view of evolutionary change that makes many cling to a surer path—the understanding of history as linear and dichotomous. This path is called progress and its line is clear. One idea, theme, discipline, proceeds through inevitable stages of growth and gets replaced with a newer idea, theme, discipline, that is inevitably more complex and better. If theorists and teachers can't believe in the inevitability of progress, the fear may be, chaos or anarchy is the only alternative. Recently, critical theory, in both its literary and rhetorical applications, has embraced postmodernism so thoroughly, and seen itself as so forward-looking, so new on the evolutionary ladder of ideas, that anything connected to older ideas about individual creativity, responsibility, or context, is seen as primitive, naive, or just plain silly. So modernism is taught as inevitably replacing the "romantic period," which had displaced the Enlightenment brought on by the Industrial Revolution and growing democracy. One would think that postmodernism would embrace models of contingency and chance, resisting as it does any models of totality, but too often it sees the past as totality rather than as contingency, and, as a theory about theories, it often rejects the past altogether. Gould reminds historians of ideas that they tend to conflate "placement in time with judgment of worth" (1989, 39)—if an idea is older, it is by definition simpler and less attractive. Gould explains that humans think this way "because of the need to believe in their own worth; such metaphors nurture our hopes for a universe of intrinsic meaning defined in our terms" (43). Our intellectual history tells us that the past must become passé in order for us to make sense of our world and our place within it. Diggins says that "The meaning of American history is to supersede itself and leave no traces of time and tradition" (1994, 18).

Romantic/pragmatic rhetoric, however, seen within Gould's perspective on evolution, and examined through the pragmatic relationship of knowledge, faith, and action, is not a fixed part of an evolutionary chain, supplanting neoclassical approaches, to be supplanted in turn by more advanced realism, or modernism, and then postmodernism. Instead, it evolved, and it evolves, but not in any linear or neatly branching way. Romantic/pragmatic rhetoric was a habit of thought that flowered among the Puritans and preachers, as well as the poets in nineteenth century America. It operates in the work of teachers in all parts of the world, in writers of science and nature, in thinkers among many disciplines. Like the Burgess Shale, it didn't supplant and wasn't supplanted. Contingency means that thought might die; chance might kill good ideas or relegate them to the pages of unread position papers or dusty lecture notes. But contingency also suggests that ideas might reform and recombine, not in some inevitable progression but in unpredictable and surprising ways and places. More like seeds blown from a dandelion than branches spreading from the trunk of a tree, romantic/pragmatic rhetoric spread far, lodged in unpredictable spots, grew roots and flowered in places, got hidden and dusted over in others, burst forth at unlikely moments. And it continues to do so.

At the end of *Walden*, Thoreau tells a story that "everyone" in New England has heard, of a beautiful, strong bug crawling out of the dry wood of an old table, brought to new life "perchance by the heat of an urn." The story becomes Thoreau's way of suggesting that good ideas don't die even if buried under layers of time:

> Who knows what beautiful and winged life, whose egg has been buried for ages under many concentric layers of woodenness in the dead dry life of society, deposited at first in the alburnum of the green and living tree, which has been gradually converted into the semblance of its well seasoned tomb—heard perchance gnawing out now for years by the astonished family of man, as they sat around the festive board—may unexpectedly come forth from amidst society's most trivial and handselled furniture, to enjoy its perfect summer life at last! (1966, 220)

In this metaphor, Thoreau practices romantic/pragmatic rhetoric—combining the natural with the scientific, beauty with utility—as he points to the continuance of ideas even when they seem dead or out of date. And, as an American romantic/pragmatic rhetorician, Thoreau affirmed a democracy of awareness. In his story, everyone can share in the beauty and power of the vision. The story he tells is both old and new, one everybody knows, one where surprising revelation may come someday at supper time. Instead of Darwinian evolution then, our metaphor for romantic/pragmatic rhetoric becomes this one of Thoreau's—the living bug, the seed dispersed and growing in corners and gardens. The metaphor explains how romantic/pragmatic rhetoric is not historical artifact or reference point but a living theory and viable method for teachers to examine, and to influence, how people come to believe and act.

SIX

CHANGING THE COURSE OF THE STREAM
Romantic/Pragmatic Perspectives on Systems

> We must keep alive the notion that history is incomplete,
> that the world is unfinished, that the future is open-ended.
> . . . If you give up that notion then there is no hope and all
> you have is sophisticated analysis. Ironic reflection. If you
> don't think what you think and what you do can make a
> difference, then the possibility of human hope wanes.
> —Cornel West, *Prophetic Thought in Postmodern Times*

> Certainly it is easier to work on trying to fit people into the
> mainstream than to try to change the course of the stream.
> —Geneva Smitherman, *Talkin' and Testifyin':*
> *The Language of Black America*

John Keating is the kind of teacher who inspires students and annoys colleagues, whose vibrant personality and engagement with ideas in his classroom guarantees both devotion and dismissal. He is the hero of the 1989 movie *Dead Poets Society*, a movie that has become one in a long line of "good teacher" movies, and a staple as a teaching tool in courses on teaching at Hepsie's university. It's a movie that would-be teachers almost universally love. It also is a movie that explores the dichotomy between the "romantic" and the "practical" that has dominated our educational theories and practices in the last century.

As Keating, Robin Williams exhibits both an impish humor and serious belief that make him an appealing if sometimes confusing teacher. Keating is idealistic—exhorting his band of Fifties upper-class prep school boys to "seize the day" and make their lives meaningful. He believes in his subject—literature—as a way to help make those lives meaningful. And he uses himself—his wit, intelligence, and bravery—to make his students rethink entrenched positions about school and life. Completely uninterested in political maneuvering, he ignores subtle warnings about the dangers of being too idiosyncratic or too critical of a system which has employed him and which will guarantee his students high places in a society of good manners and careful training. After a student commits suicide rather than face such a programmed future administered by a frightening autocratic father, Keating is blamed outright for the kind of teaching that fosters dissent and, inevitably, despair. His students, who have learned from him the romantic maxim of Thoreau and Whitman to live fully, are forced to accuse him. He leaves the school, but not before many of the boys have stood up for him, facing censure (though it's not shown and is probably not severe) from the administrator who has taken over Keating's class.

One pivotal scene depicting Keating's teaching method illustrates the reason so many young people preparing to teach see this movie as a touchstone. Keating begins a class on poetry by demonstrating the dangers of the *merely* efficient in teaching, mocking a textbook account about the proper method of arriving at a determination of a poem's worth by plotting a graph of "perfection" and "importance" and coloring in the area of intersection. This "bad teaching" is juxtaposed to Keating's method, which is to tear up these directive pages of the book, to encourage students to listen to the poem and to listen to Keating himself. Although promoting "good teaching," the approach is in fact *merely* romantic. Keating reacts rather than examines and mediates, doesn't consider consequences or the context in which his actions are placed. In fact, he loses at the end, and the repressive system wins, except for the few guerrilla fighters who may or may not go on to "make their lives extraordinary" by changing the conditions of the worlds they inhabit. It doesn't appear that there will be many of them who choose this path. As Gradin says, "However truly radical Keating's pedagogy, it remains that *Dead Poets Society* (deftly) portrays the conservative nature of education in the 1950s" (1995, 20).

This portrayal of the doomed heroic teacher appeals in the 1990s to students at all levels, those who wish they might have had such a teacher in their own schooling, those who want to be teachers like Keating. Students in Hepsie's pre-practice seminar for English majors preparing for their student teaching semester often used *Dead Poets Society* in their journals as an example of the teacher they'd like to be but never expect to be:

—Every teacher wants to be like Robin Williams, to have students love you and to make a difference. The truth is most teachers don't know how to be and never will.

—Mr. Keating is my hero. I want to be like him. I loved the part where they stood on their desks. I don't think my students would ever get down if I let them get up.

—He teaches them not to be afraid to experience and to try always to have a complete image of each aspect of life that surrounds them. Even though his idea backfired.

—I cannot wait to share parts of this movie, which is the only movie that I cry at each time I see it.

These young teachers find the character and the methods he employs in the classroom admirable, but they can't take lessons from Keating. The only message they seem to take from the movie is that the system will beat down the best and most committed teachers. "Of course he has to leave teaching," one comments; "they never let people like that stay." Young teachers often find themselves depressed rather than inspired by the portrayal of a romantic figure who walks away from the classroom and leaves it to the system once again. In the movie, the headmaster now teaching Keating's class, takes up the lesson Keating has abandoned, and begins to re-instill the method of valuing the poem by charting its relative perfection and importance.

Yet even though he fails at changing the repressive system he finds himself in, Keating does attempt to live out a romantic pragmatism in the teaching philosophy he follows. When he teaches poetry, he demonstrates the pragmatic maxim of use, by suggesting that the students' responses and the connection between poet and reader's experience determine a poem's worth, not its plotting on a chart that sets importance and perfection of style as the markers for a poem's excellence. Perhaps what moviegoers, especially hopeful teachers in training, respond to most strongly is the sense of possibility that this teacher inspires, the insistence that the individual matters and can make choices about how she lives and what she reads. But teachers need more than mythic heroes to make real differences in their classrooms. They must find ways to provoke and enact change in systematic and institutional ways. Otherwise, the view is always nostalgic—the real danger of romanticism—always wishful, always already lost.

FROM THE LOST GARDEN TO THE AGORA—
MERELY ROMANTIC TO ROMANTIC PRAGMATISM

Barbara Herrnstein-Smith's book *Contingencies of Value* describes the principle of value that Keating attempts to teach his students. Her theoretical understandings begin to give some underpinning to a new concept
of value that teachers might use to provoke the kind of change Keating
looks for in his school and in his students. A Shakespearean scholar,
Herrnstein-Smith remembers the dozens of times she has read the
sonnets, noting how fickle her fancy is as a reader: "What I at the
moment regard as favorites among the poems, I once (last week or ten
years ago) thought of as obscure, grotesque, or raw" (1988, 6). Like all
value, she asserts, "literary value is not the property of an object or of
a subject but rather the product of the dynamics of a system" (15).
The emphasis is on function, context, and the interchange of ideas
between those who are considering value, as Keating knew.

Herrnstein-Smith sees the problem of evaluation or value as one
of a conflict in ideologies between "positivistic philological scholarship and humanistic pedagogy" (18). Academics, she maintains, want
the rigor associated with science but they want as well to stay faithful
to a didactic mission—which is to "honor and preserve objects"(20).
Although evaluative criticism remains intellectually suspect, she says,
and has been so since the time of the New Criticism and the affective
fallacy, it certainly is exercised in the classroom. The headmaster of
the Wilton School in *Dead Poets Society* exemplifies this contradiction in
his reduction of poetry to scientific principles and in his insistence
that those principles will yield the same results for all readers and for
all poems.

The need to reduce scholarship to a fact-centered, valueless system derives from the impulse to objectify, and thus credit, certain kinds
of responses to texts or artifacts. Critics like Northrop Frye attempted
to remove judgments of value from academic scholarship, dismissing
as personal and thus irrelevant considerations of "taste." Frye's rejection of "taste" in *Anatomy of Criticism*, Herrnstein-Smith argues, was so
effective that he exempted it from the critical conversation "at least to
the extent of haunting a generation of literary scholars, critics, and
teachers, many of whom are still inclined to apologize for making
overt value judgments . . ." (18).

It may be true that researchers and theorists have attempted to abandon value as a consideration in criticism, although, as Herrnstein-Smith would be among the first to recognize, that attempt itself is laden with value judgments. The New Critics and those who have followed them, all those who attempt to replace the "personal" and "subjective" with "scientific" or "empirical" conclusions, assert beliefs about what counts as knowledge, how it should be organized and investigated, and how it should be presented. Further, teachers find themselves in a no less difficult position even if they try to pass along value judgments via didactic pedagogical measures such as selection of canons and curricula, exclusion of certain forms of written response, and classroom activities as lecture/discussion. Herrnstein-Smith's characterization of the problem in teaching and scholarship only scratches the surface of the issue and misdiagnoses in part both teaching and scholarship in English studies. The problem is not merely conflicting desires among academics who yearn to abandon value in their research and assert it in their teaching, but an inability to lay claim to values, belief, or ethics as the province of both scholarship and teaching. The conflict remains the same for teachers and writers with regard to value: how do we reconcile the personal response and the public understanding? How does value become a dynamic process rather than a static product?

Despite a misunderstanding about the conflict between teaching and scholarship, Herrnstein-Smith defends a method that could both provoke and sustain the kind of inquiry that might lead to scholarship and teaching not divorced from notions of value. This inquiry, continual and open, "might be expected to make its accounts internally consistent, externally connectable and amenable to continuous extension and refinement, for it is thus that the theoretical power and productivity of these accounts would be served and secured" (28). She is calling for pragmatic action, although she doesn't call it that, for interaction between individuals toward social consensus, for an understanding of context and its effect on matters of fact and value, for an assertion of practice as the test of truth. In this way, her argument would suggest, teaching and scholarship can both become more meaningful, the trap of either/or can be escaped and, most important, value can enter explicitly into theoretical and practical discussions of interpretation.

Herrnstein-Smith departs from pragmatists in her refusal to grant the possibility of cumulative knowledge or even contingent truth. But her emphasis on contingency shows how one can work away from the positivistic evolutionary metaphors that guide conceptions of reality and toward more imaginative, less stable views. Herrnstein-Smith makes the consequences of the evolutionary model explicit as she describes a new way of thinking about progress and developments: "Not only is an entity always explored under more or less different conditions, but the various explorations do not yield a simple cumulative (correct, improved, deeper, more thorough, complete) knowledge of the entity because they are not additive" (32). In other words, change does not equal progress, and simple accumulation does not result in final, or even usable, truth. Thinkers must always question, always test, individually and in concert, to come to decisions about knowledge and its value. Herrnstein-Smith, along with other theorists who attempt to rethink the fact/value split that dominates both research and teaching, suggests possibilities for making systems, such as the one that produced Mr. Keating, more responsive to the individuals who live within them. The work of this chapter will be to help teachers find usable, mediating methods in their work, so that they can do more than bemoan the fate of the heroic teacher who fights for students and almost always loses in the system.

THE TYRANNICAL MACHINE

As we've shown, many of the early romantics were fearful of systems, which they equated with the technological and mechanical, for just the reasons that Robin Williams's character in *Dead Poets Society* demonstrates. When Emerson cries out that "the machine unmans us" he expresses the deep-seated fear among the romantics that humans and human actions might be expendable in a culture that sees "advances" based primarily on technological progress and the growth of systematic knowledge. That fear, expressed by most of the nineteenth-century romantics in one form or another, was not unfounded. As Callahan demonstrates, the systematic and the technical all but replaced the individual and the contextual in institutions like education that seemed especially vulnerable to charges of inefficiency and "romantic" impracticality. The scientific, the verifiable, the efficient, above all the systematic, became highly prized in schools, where money seems always tight and progress always seems so ineffable. Schools developed enormous systems based on models of efficient workplaces, and schools at secondary and higher education levels operate with those models today.

Some fear that too much emphasis on the individual or the contextual might lead to chaos, a lack of system at all. This problem, the fear of a lack of system, is described by a graduate student in a seminar Hepsie recently taught in romantic rhetoric: "Many see the beauty of meeting particular situations individually, but have a problem with what they perceive to be a lack of set principles to live by. They see the application of 'romantic rhetoric' as impractical in light of the realities of education systems in America." He, and many other students in the seminar, attest to the continuing belief that romantic ideology and pragmatic experiment are simply impractical in a world of "realities." Those realities, for these students and for teachers in public schools, include illiteracy and attrition, failed homes and failed classrooms, drugs and violence and poverty. In such a context the word *romantic* seems almost mocking, and the word *pragmatic* seems merely cynical.

"We regress instead of progressing. We are unable to embrace those whom we need to embrace. We are unable to even reach out to those whom we need to reach out towards." Philip, another seminar participant, comments about the culture and its implications for education and strikes a hopeless note. He continues with what he sees as the solution to the difficulty: "Both West and Peirce recognize the necessity of love for their vision of human progress, for the expulsion of exploitation and oppression from human societies. Love is a bridge which we build—it is not discovered—without which romantic rhetoric is impossible."

This insistence on the recognition of common and reciprocal humanity through the agency of a rigorous, rather than sentimentalized, principle of love is something that students in the seminar, who are teachers themselves, found to be a thread in the work they read and in their own work as teachers. To recognize the human dimension does not mean that systems are ignored, that technology, whether of the railroad or the computer or the standardized test, is to be simply dismissed as in- or anti-human. As Freire says of solutions to social and cultural problems, "the answer does not lie in the rejection of the machine but rather in the humanization of man" (1990, 35). People, women as well as men, must come to a realization of their responsibilities in community; they must educate one another to free one another by providing new perspectives, developing new knowledge. They must see systems for what they are, not truths, not unchangeable entities, but simple aids to accomplishing human goals.

Still, Freire's words suggest that while systems may not be evil, humans' responses to them make systems vulnerable to evil. Writing about the newly popular Ph.D. degree in 1903, William James sounds frighteningly contemporary as he observes how systems uncriticized and unremarked become monstrous. Called "The Ph.D. Octopus," this essay begins by recounting the case of a Harvard graduate student whose brilliance secured him a good teaching job in philosophy which was rescinded as soon as the governors of the institution made the "awful discovery" that he didn't hold the Ph.D. The faculty at Harvard assured the university of the student's excellence but were informed that quality "per se of the man signified nothing in this connection, and that three magical letters were the thing seriously required" (1960, 1111). James uses this case to argue that system, the institutionalizing of individual case, can often harbor evil consequences: "The institutionalizing on a large scale of any natural combination of need and motive always tends to run into technicality and to develop a tyrannical Machine with unforeseen powers of exclusion and corruption" (1113).

Despite his plea for American universities to come to their senses, James might have foreseen the day when no one would be admitted to full participation in university teaching and intellectual life without those three magical letters attached to the name; the Ph.D. is today more than ever the passport to work, as a professional equal, in the academy. And as he no doubt also saw, the implications of the Ph.D. octopus reach far beyond university education. The demand for certification, the requirement of rule, separate and apart from individual or local case, has increased mightily since James's time. Thus the warning about specialization in "The American Scholar"—"a stomach and elbow, but never a man"—and the echo in James in the "decidedly grotesque tendency" of systems to ignore human reality and potential are foreshadowings of both Taylor's dictum to put "system first," and Freire's and West's warnings about the dangers of systems.

Václav Havel, poet and president of newly democratic Czechoslovakia, has written eloquently and often about the dialogue between the human and the systematic in a world that often calls for people to become, in Havel's words, "prisoners of their own skepticism" (1990, 177). Havel calls for a change in systems and, especially, the way people conceive them. Like James and Freire, Havel doesn't excoriate systems themselves, but concentrates on revealing how easily systems are led away from the essential component and rationale for them, the human dimension:

> Man must in some way come to his senses. He must extricate himself from this terrible involvement in both the obvious and the hidden mechanisms of totality, from consumption to repression, from advertising to manipulation through television. He must rebel against his role as a helpless cog in the gigantic and enormous machinery hurtling God knows where. He must discover again, within himself, a deeper sense of responsibility toward the world, which means responsibility toward something higher than himself. Modern science has realized this (though not the proprietors of "the scientific world view"), but it cannot find a remedy. The power to awaken this new responsibility is beyond its reach; such a thing can be resolved neither scientifically nor technically. (11)

Havel insists that the immediate and the local and the human provide the only possibility for confronting what West calls the "nihilisms and cynicisms" that make up so much of the current cultural and intellectual climate. People must have a say in the systems they work within: "the most important thing is for economic units to maintain—or rather renew—their relationship with individuals, so that the work those people perform has human substance and meaning, so that people can see into how the enterprise they work for works, have a say in that, and assume responsibility for it" (15).

Work must be meaningful; and the landscape be protected; the "secret inventiveness of nature, its infinite variety, the inscrutable complexity of its interconnections be honored." Most important for Havel is that a real sense of community must govern individuals' actions, a responsibility that would prevent systems from becoming tyrannical machines. A person must "relinquish something of his private interest in favor of the interest of the community, the general interest. Without such a mentality, even the most carefully considered project aimed at altering systems will be for naught" (17–18). Havel's perception that individual interest is, and must be, tied to common good is one that the Puritans in the New England villages would have understood.

SCHOOLS AS SYSTEMS

The acceptance of the idea that system itself is immutable is responsible for many of the ills that beset school systems from lower grades
to universities. Practice teachers in the schools, filled with plans and
ideals, too often find themselves scorned for thinking they can "beat
the system." Sharon, a student teacher and now a second-year English teacher, says: "They let you know, in the faculty lounge, that
your ideas are what the university teaches and not what the real world
of school is. . . . And the real world of school is to obey the rules, even
if you don't know why." Evan, a student teacher who didn't complete
student teaching the first time around because his performance was
judged unsatisfactory after only three weeks, was a student whose
qualities would have appeared to make him a nearly ideal new teacher.
Bright, articulate, a cooperative group member and a fine writer, Evan
also possessed a strong and considered desire to help nurture the literacy of students he would teach. He had already taught international
students in the Philippines, and he had clearly articulated beliefs about
how to value the knowledge and experience students bring with them
to a class and how to use students' expertise to provoke new knowledge. Yet his tenure at his high school had been judged by all concerned a disaster.

His biggest failure by his cooperating teacher's account, and his
own, was expressed as an inability to confront the organizational and
management details of the job. "I guess it started when I realized there
were so many jobs to do all at once," he says. When asked, the first job
he cites is secretarial: "I didn't learn quickly how to mark the roll. I
didn't realize that was such a big deal in the system." Even worse than
his lack of ability to do these kinds of bookkeeping chores was his
unwillingness to take seriously some of the tasks that most teachers
and administrators in the system performed as a matter of course.
Evan felt some of the requests made of him, like the correct method
for attendance taking, or the procedure for dealing with tardiness, or
grading with percentages every assignment, were useless, or worse,
wrongheaded. "Some things you're told to do seem pointless," he says,
"but you can't say that."

We recount Evan's experience not to suggest that rules, systems,
organization, are not appropriate or necessary in the educational setting. It is to say, however, that teachers and, especially, administrators

sometimes become so embedded in the rules of a system that they forget that systems are designed solely to support those who work within them. Evan's failure is a failure of a system that couldn't recognize his considerable strengths because it couldn't get beyond the system's prescriptions. Happily for education and for Evan, he re-enrolled in student teaching in an open school with a strong and innovative teacher and is now teaching and thriving in a high school where minority enrollment is about 80 percent and where many of his ideas about the strengths of diverse perspectives are welcomed.

WHEN THE SYSTEM BREAKS

Although Evan's school system story has a happy ending, many stories of the inattention of the educational system to the lives of those who are a part of it don't end so positively. Jonathan Kozol offers a sobering perspective on failure in books that document the unresponsiveness of education to the needs of students, especially African American students. His *Savage Inequalities* is a stunning indictment of public education and its attempt to make education available and equal for all. Kozol first taught in Boston in 1964, in a poor, segregated school that was so crowded that his fourth graders shared the auditorium with a group practicing for the Christmas play, and then among students who had endured a succession of substitute teachers all year long. He was not surprised when the children scored poorly on literacy achievement tests. In 1988 Kozol revisited schools in Massachusetts and elsewhere to see what the effects of integration might have been. He discovered that not only did schools remain segregated, with urban schools predominantly black, but also they were so poorly maintained that it felt like an ugly armed camp to be in them. "Looking around some of these inner city schools where filth and disrepair were worse than anything I'd seen in 1964, I often wondered why we would agree to let our children go to school in places where no politician, or business CEO would dream of working" (1991, 28).

Kozol's anger at a system that would fail so completely its children is evident in his call for change. He holds accountable officials and administrators, education personnel and ordinary citizens, for not demanding that the system of education be made to answer to its claims of equality and belief in possibility among its young. The statistics he provides on per-pupil expenditure and the defeat he chronicles among the teachers of the poor and disadvantaged reveal how great the disparity is between rich and poor, black and white. At one point, he visits a poor ghetto school where the students are reading Paul Laurence Dunbar. The school is in such disrepair that holes in the walls and ceiling leave the structural brick exposed. There are no shades on the windows, and students and teacher squint despite the torn construction paper that's been taped up to shade them. The teacher asks students to read aloud. They read haltingly. Then the teacher asks the children what "the poet means or what the imagery conveys." There is no response at first. Then a young man named Victor raises his hand: "'The poem is about the ancient days of slavery,' he says. 'The bird destroys himself because he can't escape the cage.' 'Why does he sing?' the teacher asks. 'He sings out of the longing to be free.'" After the class, when Kozol questions her, she says that "forty, maybe forty-five percent of this group will graduate" (103).

Kozol's newest book, *Amazing Grace*, broadens his critique of educational inequity to include society at large, and his response in the 11 December 1995 issue of *Time* to the death of abused child Eliza Izquierdo illustrates dramatically the argument he makes in that book. American society suffers from a moral contradiction in its ideals and actions, a contradiction that is embodied in social programs that are never given enough money to make them work and easy hand-wringing about the problems with family, community, social service agency and bureaucracy that translate for most of the American public into inaction or punitive action in the form of the vote. Kozol writes in that article: "Then the next time an election comes we vote against the taxes that might make prevention programs possible, while favoring increased expenditures for prisons to incarcerate the children who survive the worst that we have done to them and grow up to be dangerous adults" (1995b, 96).

Kozol recognizes that the children whose futures are lost are in some way perceived to be "not ours." Most of the victims of modern ghetto life are very poor black and Hispanic children. Claiming that this inaction and inattention of most of the public to the plight of these children constitute a serious breach of America's notion of itself and damage "our collective soul," Kozol challenges readers to refuse to exempt themselves on the grounds of distance or color or region: "The more we know, the harder it becomes to grant ourselves exemption" (96). Knowledge, he tells us, carries with it both power and responsibility. We—parents, teachers, congressional representatives—can no longer ignore our failures as a society that eventuate in violence and death.

And yet despite continual documented evidence, like Kozol's, of failure of administrative inequity and irresponsibility, the system—government, agency, school board—continues. It continues to rely on its rules, and its policy statements, its self-congratulatory reviews, its inbred quality control measures, its meaningless statistics. As one of the most important systems with regard to the young and their ability to participate in their society, the educational system bears special responsibility for the failures of so many of its poorest members. Its inability to create equity or sites for integration is damning. As Kozol notes, education systems, and government at all levels, continue to view segregation as "a past injustice that had been sufficiently addressed" (1995a, 3). And this inability is part of its general refusal to be responsible and responsive to situations and contexts. Racial injustice grows from the institution's continuing denial of its human responsibility.

If educational systems fail to meet their responsibility to society's need for equity and racial equality, they fail consistently on small, immediate human matters as well, and these smaller instances have devastating consequences that simply underscore what critics like Kozol describe. On 11 October 1994, Kevin (a fictitious name), a sophomore at a large high school in Greensboro, North Carolina, was suspended from school for two days for smoking a cigarette on campus. The rule was clear though inconsistently administered, given the number of high school students who smoked in the parking lot and the sidewalks and streets just off school grounds. The day after his suspension, Kevin returned to school, shot and slightly wounded the assistant principal who had suspended him, and then turned the gun on himself. He died at the hospital several hours later.

Kevin's is obviously a more complicated story than its bare outlines would suggest. Kevin was what popular magazines euphemistically call a "troubled teen." He had been unruly several times before this incident, had spent time in an alternative school, and had been sent back to the high school warned that any further trouble would result in a permanent suspension. No one knows what went through his mind when the assistant principal refused to consider the details of his case as he meted out punishment. Kevin's anger and despair, however, are documented in the action he took with a gun he retrieved from his home where it had been locked up, but of course was available.

Some blame this unhappy situation on what they might in another day have called "mollycoddling" students, and what they disparage now with the term "self-esteem." An editorial in the *Greensboro News and Record* takes this stance. Managing editor David DuBuisson begins his column, called "Can Our Public Schools Ever be Liberated from the Curse of Self-Esteem?" this way: "If I had to sum up my misgivings about school in two words, they would be 'self' and 'esteem.' Together they've become the mantra of the modern American educator. The term epitomizes the essential difference between school then and now" (1994, 13). DuBuisson's point is that self-esteem is sheer pride "in the Biblical sinful sense," giving students an unrealistic, unhealthy, and overly positive image of their abilities and accomplishments. Self-esteem, he believes, is responsible for students' increasingly poor achievement on national tests of intelligence and skill: "Without stress, without struggle, failure and self-doubt, there can be no achievement worth mentioning" (13).

It's clear that Kevin didn't suffer from an overload of self-esteem, and neither does the majority of students in schools no matter what their scores on tests, their grade point averages, their designation in education's rigidly assigned class structure as "average," "college prep," or "vocational." DuBuisson's editorial is a wrongheaded account of the causes of failure within a system, one that puts the blame in exactly the wrong place, on teachers and students within a system that refuses to grant most of its members much measure of esteem at all.

Whatever else it is, this small story's message is failure. Teenagers seem to be increasingly alienated and angry; schools seem increasingly to be unable to do anything to abate the tide of violence and despair that grips the lives of so many of their clientele. Where is the failure? The pragmatists would suggest that failure lies in the refusal to inquire into the system and its rules and to act on the results of that inquiry. Failure will also attend endeavors that refuse to take local contexts into account, and nothing will change until connections between individuals and communities are recognized and employed. The high school in question is not an exception to the rule of most schools, most systems in fact, in and out of education. Those who work in systems, especially those of us who have prospered within them, have been content to divorce individual need from community interest, and have ignored or actively downplayed the links between individual and system. Administrators, teachers, all those with power in educational settings, have too often and for too long allowed ourselves the mistaken but easy belief that evenhandedness means justice. The assistant principal no doubt believed that following the system's rules, without regard to the individual case, served the best interests of all—his employer, parents, the community. But the individual case is always significant in a system. This particular case was about emotional distress, a troubled present, a "good kid" past, and—perhaps the single most pertinent factor for Kevin—an infraction that was so minute that it was committed daily and consistently by scores of students, and some teachers. The administration of justice, divorced from the individual, human instance, was unjust. And injustice often leads to violence. How much responsibility should administrators be allowed to have in administering the system's rules? How much should they be required to have? How much should a system administrator know about education and adolescent psychology? How much should he be required to make use of? How much is an administrator a representative of a system? How much a representative of the humans who comprise the system? The sad case of Kevin demonstrates James's point in tragic detail: when inevitability and not contingency guide a system it becomes tyrannical. When objectivity and myth rather than fallibility and recognition of human judgment determine outcomes, injustice is the result.

How can the myth of the immutable system be altered and individuals be helped to see their responsibilities in human terms? What this book has been calling romantic/pragmatic rhetoric is a method toward the end of promoting in organic and real ways a rationale for belief, in the individual and in the community. It's a method for systematizing that belief so that it becomes continually tested and rethought and continually responsive to changing contexts. Administrators are not the most powerful players or agents of change in this scene, even though in the rigid hierarchy of education they appear to be. It's faculty, who act on their beliefs in the multiple conversations they carry on in and out of the classroom, who can determine whether systems will answer to the human interest or not.

In this next chapter, we examine some teachers at work, pragmatic/romantic rhetoricians who understand the need for an answer to the pragmatic question, "What difference does it make?" These teachers, separated by circumstance, by time, by locale, and even perhaps by philosophical orientation, help other teachers be able to answer yes to Berthoff's question "Is teaching still possible?"

SEVEN

WHAT DIFFERENCE DOES IT MAKE?
Romantic / Pragmatic Rhetoric in Action

> Theory is not inherently healing, liberatory, or revolution-
> ary. It fulfills this function only when we ask that it do so
> and direct our theorizing toward this end. . . . The posses-
> sion of a term does not bring a process or practice into
> being.
>
> —bell hooks, *Teaching to Transgress*

> Fear nearly keeps me from writing "love" here. . . Fear of
> being perceived as too soft, too romantic. Fear of being
> decidedly "uncool" and utterly dismissable in the current
> academic climate. Fear even of being somehow untrue to
> my own affinity to the big cold ideas of critical theory and
> antifoundationalism. . . . If there is a lesson in this back-
> ward glance, it is this: fear can prevent us from loving. I
> now see that maintaining high standards and holding stu-
> dents responsible for their work and for reaching their po-
> tential is a crucial part of loving them.
>
> —Chris, journal, graduate seminar
> in Romantic/Pragmatic Rhetoric

Like Thoreau's "beautiful and winged life," buried under the "wood-
enness" of "dead, dry society" but bursting forth in unexpected places
and times, and like the Burgess Shale discoveries, romantic/pragmatic
rhetoric is alive and active in many places, though too often seen as
the exception rather than as a real possibility. In this chapter we present
examples of romantic/pragmatic rhetoric at work, in theory and in
practice, in order to argue for the possibility of hope for real change in
education. The philosophy we illustrate here is active, restless, imperfect, hopeful, and brave. Dewey argued that a philosophy worthy of
the name must be connected both to agendas for real action and to
responsibility for the consequences of that action: "A philosophy which
was conscious of its own business and province would then perceive

139

that it is an intellectualized wish, an aspiration subjected to rational discrimination and tests, a social hope reduced to a working program of action, a prophecy of the future, but one disciplined by serious thought and knowledge" (1982, 43). Romantic/pragmatic rhetoric, as we have shown, has not been named as a philosophy, and some of its practitioners may not be "conscious" of the roots of their methods and beliefs; however, what follows does, indeed, embody "social hope" and a "working program," however unfinished, for change.

THE ROMANTIC/PRAGMATIC CLASSROOM

Into the high school: He sings out of a longing to be free

Bill Buczinksy is a second-year English teacher in the same school where Kevin committed suicide last year. He teaches five classes, two honors ninth grade classes, one "regular" ninth grade, and two "standard" ninth grade sections. These last sections are filled with students who for one reason or another could be labeled "at risk." Students are more likely to be poor, to come from dangerous neighborhoods. Many—a disproportionately large number—are black. Several students speak English as a second language. Two are physically handicapped, one with a leg brace and an arm brace that Bill will adjust to aid the student's writing. One student stutters noticeably with each sentence. They are students who are in danger of getting lost in a system that seems often to have despaired of helping them. It is an old classroom with large windows and seats ranged around on three sides. Bill never sits. He jokes as the bell rings, takes roll quickly, cues up a tape, writes on the board, answers questions, gives directions all at once it seems. There are twenty-six students.

Hepsie is sitting in Bill's class to observe. She sits on one side of the room, watching Bill, who walks among the students as he begins the class, laughing as he talks: "Guys, if you could do a favor for me here and get started. While you're preparing for class to begin I'm going to cue up something for you." "Notice what Andrew has on his head." "Yes, I see you have that notebook open. Good." He's speaking fast and moving as he talks, commanding their attention with his good will. He puts on a recording of some classical music, passes out copies of the poem they will read and discuss today, and asks students to begin to read. It is Paul Laurence Dunbar's poem "Sympathy." "You may know this poem," Bill says. "You may know what the poet feels like. Before we do anything else, I want you to take five minutes and think about it. Write for five minutes. Do you ever feel trapped like the guy in the poem? Do you know why the caged bird sings?"

The scene is eerily like the one Kozol describes in *Savage Inequalities* where students read Dunbar and comment on freedom. But here in this class, the theory that supports the reading of the poem is evident in every aspect of the class and clear even in the small exchange above. There is theory about literature, about poetry and about reading, a belief that Bill signals in his choice that suggests the power of reading, its universality, its connection and relevance to students' experience, its openness to meaning and significance. There is writing theory evident. Writing is supported by reading; writing can be shared in a communal experience; writing works in informal, in-class, nonpressured ways. There is learning theory. Reading and writing are acts of interpretation; students have knowledge to share; knowledge is extended as it is linked to other kinds of knowledge. And there is pedagogical theory that values the social, the interactive, the dialogue between teacher and student.

Students, most of them, write quickly. A few stumble, tear up paper. One or two have trouble writing at all. Bill moves to the young man with the leg brace and incomplete control over his arm motions. He pats him on the shoulder, makes a joke. The student smiles and sheepishly looks at his blank page. Students understand the messages Bill sends, but he makes them explicit: "I'm giving you time here because I want you to think about how much you know about what our poet is talking about."

There are more or less constant interruptions during this time. Announcements come on the loudspeaker, a student arrives to get Bill to sign her homeroom slip, someone from the office brings forms. The interruptions bother some of the students; others don't seem to notice. Once in a while someone will "shush" someone else as one offers a comment or laughs.

When everybody is finished or close enough, Bill asks students to read aloud their responses. Predictably, they begin with characterizations of school as a time to feel caged. School is a prison. Bill talks about rules, about breaking them. He tells a story about a student he's seen eating lunch off campus. He tells them what he's said to the rule breaker: "You look just like a kid I know who's a junior. So he wouldn't be here at Taco Bell because only seniors can do that of course." The students all laugh. "Why the rule about going off campus?" Bill says. "Because some people won't come back." "When is it OK to break a rule in the system?" Students ask this question but don't answer it. They are finding the connections between what they've written about being caged and the discussion about breaking and making rules.

As students talk and respond, read or tell what they've written, Bill watches to see who is waiting to speak, who is quiet but ready. He does this casually, calmly, seeing the whole class, attentive to both speaker at the moment and listeners. A young woman from Colombia speaks about being caged in a culture where she's not allowed to wear long hair at her school, and the other students whistle. The students ask other questions about her school and her hometown in Bogotá. The conversation moves to several students who sit close together and begin complaining of being in prison at home with parents who don't trust them to set their own curfews or who don't like their friends. One or two comment on being imprisoned in their jobs, where dress codes and hours keep them trapped.

One young man has been quietly following the discussion, looking down every so often at his paper to check it, offering a comment as others have spoken up. Finally, he raises his hand and Bill catches it. Ron begins to speak, but Bill stops him. "Why don't you read?" he says. Ron reads: "It's bad when school is a prison or when your house is. When the walls around you trap you. But that's not the worst thing." Ron tells about his life at home. His grandmother won't let him go shoot baskets in the evening at the park because "just last week they held up some kids down there." And how he won't walk to the store anymore because there's been three drive-bys in the last month. "You should feel free when you're outside in the air. It's the worst thing when your own neighborhood, everything around you makes you feel like you're in a prison."

Bill asks someone to read "Sympathy" aloud now, and then again. He looks at Ron and says, "Ron knows 'what the caged bird feels, alas.'" Ron laughs. "I wouldn't use 'alas.'" Everybody begins to talk at once, but time—alas—is up. Students gather up their books, a few pat Ron on the back as they leave. One girl who has complained about the prison of her house, a girl who stutters and has haltingly read her piece, stops to speak to Bill about her response.

During the course of talking about the poem and eliciting students' reactions, Bill has taught rhyme scheme and rhythm, asking students to identify patterns. He has used the words *mood, persona, metaphor, stanza*. He has used the words of students themselves, their "generative words" to use Freire's phrase, as well as words he has brought to the conversation, his own generative words that will become part of the larger conversation of the class.

Bill's classroom exhibits more than quiet change, more than the "thinking globally/acting locally" slogan that has influenced many university professors who teach education and advocate quiet subversiveness in a system that seems to thwart positive change. Bill's class instead is a stunning example of romantic/pragmatic rhetoric, a careful and real use of the tensions between individual and community, between the world of the text and the world outside it, between Bill as a teacher and as a human, between belief and a system operating on doubt.

As university teachers, teachers at both college and high school levels, our work is to translate the lesson of Bill's classroom into theory and method for teachers to use themselves. Multiculturalism is not simply a desideratum for textbooks or for faculty personnel; it is not simply another educational buzzword for managing students. Bill's class teaches the lesson that teachers must know the lives of their students, must hear and learn from them, use them to provoke new understandings about everything the class reads and writes. As a teacher responsible for other teachers, Hepsie needs to name for them what she's experienced as an observer in that class, to name the romantic/ pragmatic rhetoric the teacher uses, and to name as well the oppression of these students in a repressive and oppressive system. Bill's class forces an examination of uncomfortable truths about our society and calls teachers of teachers to action.

The Primary School and the Administrator: Revolutionary Implications

Stories of romantic/pragmatic teachers abound once you begin looking for them, once you know how to name them. Deborah Meier is the principal and founder of a small elementary and middle school in East Harlem that has become famous for its success in a neighborhood of poverty and neglect. Called the Central Park East Schools, these institutions have been hailed as a miracle in public school education.

Her brand of romantic pragmatism has made this experiment work in an enormous public school system, one that like most large systems, has difficulty making innovation possible.

In the book that tells the story of this innovation, *The Power of Their Ideas*, Meier discusses her first inkling of what public education really meant as she describes herself as a beginning kindergarten teacher in a depressed area public school in Chicago: "It was only after I had begun to teach that public rhetoric gave even lip service to the notion that all children could and should be the inventors of their own theories, critics of other people's ideas, analyzers of evidence and makers of their own personal marks on this most complex world. It's an idea that has revolutionary implications. If we take it seriously" (1995, 4).

Authentic collaboration and mediation are difficult, as the pragmatists found and as Meier's experience underscores: "It's not surprising that so many families, so many teachers, and so many politicians are looking for an escape, urging us to retreat to an imagined past where everyone succeeded—with their McGuffey readers, teacher-proof daily lesson plans—and desks that faced forward all in a row— or to opt out altogether into their separate ethnic or religious enclaves. We're not accustomed to recognize the power of each other's ideas; it's easier to take flight" (11). Meier and her colleagues, however, refuse the easy path of flight from difficulty and insist on a means of achieving a progressive education that is both child and community centered.

The work Meier has done in her school is both highly theoretical and deeply tangible. School personnel consciously combine reflection and action, theory and practice, in their work together and with parents. Meier gives a lot of power to the teachers in the school, understanding that adults need to feel power over their own work lives, that real community can never be fostered without that sense of shared power. "Without a radical departure from a more authoritarian model," she says, "one strips the key parties of the respect which lies at the heart of democratic practice of good schooling" (38). Mediation is always required: "Personal autonomy and communal decision making didn't always go well together"(39). And conflict can be useful for allowing differences to help negotiate new paths of learning and method.

Beyond changing the power structure to give teachers authority and parents responsibility, Meier designed the school to be small, where teachers see only forty students a day, and see the same students for two years. Students help design their work, help make decisions about all kinds of matters from the time school begins to the paint on the walls in their classroom. School is open after hours for special programs, and standards for excellence come from within. A portfolio system of review is an interdisciplinary and several-years-long venture, where students compile, revise, review and present work to a board composed of faculty, parents, and other members of the community. Always there is the notion of respect and responsibility, of belief and expectation that guides all the decisions made by faculty and students alike. Meier sounds very much like Kozol as she writes, "[G]ive to the disadvantaged what you have always offered to those who have money to buy the best, which is mostly a matter of respect" (57). The teacher who's a romantic/pragmatic rhetorician recognizes the "power of their ideas," all those who are speakers and listeners in the classroom, the students in the desks, the teacher herself, the writers of the texts the class reads, the newspaper headlines, the parents, the principal, the latest movie, the new TV show. All of their voices affect how the class makes knowledge, and the romantic/pragmatic teacher knows she can't afford to exclude any of them if she wishes to nurture her students' interpretive power.

Meier's belief is no mushy romantic doctrine, nothing like the kind of self-indulgent navel-gazing or silly false-esteem measures that Winterowd accuses the composition class of fostering: "If we want children to be caring and compassionate, then we must provide a place for growing up in which effective care is feasible. Caring and compassion are not soft mushy goals. They are part of the hard core of subjects we are responsible for teaching" (63). Part of this caring involves nurturing the spirit of teachers and students alike, time for reflection, time for staff to talk with each other and with parents. And it involves safety: "[T]eachers in a small school setting know when students are likely to explode and can respond rapidly. They offer what metal detectors and guards cannot: the safety and security of being where you are known well by people who care for you" (112). Had Kevin, the high school student in North Carolina, been in such a school, his story might not have ended so tragically.

Romantic pragmatism insists that feeling is part of reason, that it is in fact inefficient to fail with so many of the students in high schools, who leave without graduating, or without learning. It embraces uncertainties, "the very elements that make teaching and learning such a lively business," as Meier's colleague Alice Selectsky writes in Meier's book (60). It believes in experimentation and in the cultivation of new habits of mind, habits that require thoughtful response rather than mindless acceptance. Posted on bulletin boards in classrooms, the habits of mind embody and enact the habits of inquiry that romantic pragmatism encourages:

Romantic/Pragmatic Inquiry	Meier's Habits of Mind
Observation/Reflection	*How do you know what you know?*
Testing/Belief	*What's your evidence?*
Connection/Mediation	*How and where does what you have learned fit in?*
Possibility	*Could things have been otherwise?*
Contingency/Community	*Who cares?*
Consequence/Action	*What difference does it make?*

Meier's school is a dramatic demonstration of how romantic pragmatism works in real school settings. It is, as Dewey says, "a working program of action," a "social hope disciplined by serious thought and knowledge."

The college classroom: Is it possible to teach English so that we stop killing one another?

Mary Rose O'Reilly is a Quaker. And her book *The Peaceable Classroom* is, unsurprisingly, about pacifism. It is also about how to operate from belief, how to teach to make a difference, how to test conclusions, and how to use consequences to initiate action. The book is both practical guide to teachers who would teach literacy—of all kinds, to all ages— and theoretical rationale for teachers who would understand the premises of classroom actions. It traces O'Reilly's life as a teacher, her growing consciousness of her responsibility to put her ethics into classroom practice, and her growing knowledge of how to do so.

　　She begins with an account of her first teaching job at a school for elementary school children with emotional and behavioral disorders, a school she calls "Black Hole." The experience with that school, where the principal was rumored to "knock the kids around a little," led her eventually to question the moral ambiguities that allow teachers not to question authority because we "were all too busy trying to survive and minimize the damage the kids could do to each other." She realizes that many of the teachers including herself had been slapped or brutalized themselves, assuming without questioning: "that went with growing up in lower middle class culture (and other cultures as well, as I now know)" (1993, 3).

The move from the Black Hole school to teaching first year composition at a large university didn't alter O'Reilly's resolve to help students not to damage one another. She enrolls in a graduate seminar where the professor asks, "Is it possible to teach English so that people stop killing one another?" The question seems almost funny, but spoken at the height of the Vietnam War, when freshmen who failed were drafted, it made a macabre kind of sense. And to O'Reilly, years afterward, with many classroom experiences behind her, it seems an essential question to ask. Her book is the method she employs to attempt to answer "yes" to her professor and to herself.

One of her ways to answer "yes" takes into consideration the value of what she calls "silence and slow time"; she suggests that most college syllabi are overcrowded, that teachers rush through too many texts in order to "cover" literary and historical periods, and finally, that what learners and teachers need is more "white space" around texts in order to contemplate, take in, discuss, and reflect on the connections between what's being taught and everyone's lived experience, as well as the implications for the future (104–5).

Written as a counter to the "little acts of violence" that make up teaching and schooling, she asks the pragmatic question, "What if we were to take seriously the possibility that students have a rich and authoritative inner life and tried to nourish rather than negate it?" (152). The process of reflection and connection depends on the group negotiating ideas, telling and listening to stories that value the individual experience. The book is about the romantic belief in the self and in possibilities and about the pragmatic consideration of testing and consequences. Through valuing the variety of experience and considering "compassion as a mode of critical inquiry," O'Reilly gives teachers hope for making real change in the classes they direct. A nonviolent pedagogy, she shows, is a pedagogy of inclusion rather than elitism; it is a pedagogy of mediation. It is, in Freire's terms, a pedagogy of hope.

Marsha Holmes's peaceable classroom: Wake Forest University,
First Year Composition, 6 October 1995

Marsha is working with her students on the issue of violence in society. Many of the essays in the reader she has selected deal in one way or another with violence—racial, cultural, gendered violence. This decision in itself comes from Marsha's pragmatic romanticism, for she has just completed a dissertation on epideictic rhetoric and the war eulogy as its primary example. Marsha argues in the dissertation that occasional rhetoric does much more than reinforce existing beliefs; like any language use, it is embedded in concepts of action. Thus, war eulogies, like any other rhetoric, do something to hearers in the way of provoking them to action. As a pacifist, Marsha is concerned that we understand the active dimensions of the kind of ceremonial war rhetoric our culture engages in. And she understands that epideictic occasions abound for students, who often see the work they do in composition class as merely ceremonial, with total emphasis given to the forms and the occasions that produce them. The analysis or argument paper, with prescribed length requirements and number of sources, is quite familiar to students, and for many sums up what writing in school consists of. Yet, like war eulogies and other "ceremonial" writing, the composition class essay fosters behaviors and patterns of thought about how knowledge gets made, and student writers are active participants in shaping those forms.

She has made use of Mary Rose O'Reilly's book in her own, suggesting that O'Reilly provides a method to translate belief in the possibilities of peace to classroom activity. Marsha's dissertation analyzes in part how groups, responding to one another's writing and to important issues that come from their reading and experience, can function to promote peaceful, that is ameliorative, action. Her historical look at epideictic rhetoric and its contemporary examples in presidential speeches and other ceremonial moments, reinforces the perception that the rhetoric of the occasion carries intent and motivates action.

This class meeting, occurring during mid semester after she has completed her dissertation, becomes Marsha's attempt to make good on her theoretical assertions about ceremonial rhetoric and a pedagogy of collaboration and peaceful interaction. In this course, she has used writing about violence as a central theme and has attempted to make the issue of violence become more than a ceremonial prompt for students' writing, and more than a generalized accounting for violence in society in students' written responses. Marsha wants students to realize what difference it makes to investigate this issue as more than an academic exercise.

The class

Hepsie arrives late and sits in a desk slightly apart from the large circle of students grouped around a table that takes up nearly the entire room. It is a narrow room and the table and chairs nearly fill it, so that it's difficult to walk around. Marsha stands at one end, a small blackboard behind her. On the other three walls are bulletin boards with photographs and articles about the contributions of African Americans to American culture. The students have been reading essays that explore the reasons for violence in American culture. They have looked at news articles, and they have written personal accounts of learning about violence in movies. Today they begin with a question each one has asked about violence, a question Marsha has asked them to write down and which they read as they go around the room. Some of the questions are: What lies at the core of violence? Will it continue to grow? When weren't we violent? How do male rituals, marking stages in the movement from boy to man, reinforce and continue violence? Is violence necessary? The questions come quickly, obviously proceeding from the reading they've been doing as well as on earlier observations, and students nod as they find themselves relating what one has said to another.

Marsha asks her students to consider these questions in terms of the drafts of essays they are composing on the role of and solution to violence. As she begins to discuss the drafts, she describes a potential draft of her own, describing a project she'd like to do that would investigate the reactions of students in the dining hall watching as the verdict was read in the O. J. Simpson trial. She has paid attention to people's reactions, she says, and white and African American viewers vary widely in their responses to the trial's verdict. She brings in a newspaper article that reinforces the findings she has made at the Student Union. She has written the writer's triangle on the board, and asks the students how she might introduce her study. "You're trying to get us to make some connections in our papers too," one student laughs. And she nods. "I want what you're doing to be real work," she says; "I want it to matter."

The class begins to break up into groups where each member shares a draft and asks questions of the others. As a class, they have talked about the bell hooks essay they've just read on black violence; they've put Burke's pentad on the board as a way to think about motives; one student has brought up Freire's concept of oppressor and oppressed as a way to get into a topic about race and violence. Now they begin to talk to one another, while Marsha moves around from group to group listening and offering an occasional comment. She pauses to ask the class to consider the writer's notes since they tell readers what writers are looking for help with.

The group Hepsie is sitting with talks quickly and energetically. "We can do revision on this stuff before we get together again." "Sunday afternoon after my parents leave. You know it's parents' weekend." One of the writer's notes given to the other group members reads in part: "I think I used most of the ideas as I revised. Please check to make sure the main point is here. I was trying to distinguish between friendly play and real violence. It may be that I don't have enough evidence to make that point (?)—Chip." They write on one another's papers, offer Hepsie one to read, and ask questions and offer suggestions as they read. It's clear that they take the task of revision to be "real work" and not just filling in the blanks of group assignment. Marsha gathers them briefly to ask if there are questions or problems that anyone needs to address; a few make appointments to see her. They say good-bye for the weekend.

Like Bill, Mary Rose, and a host of other teachers we could name, Marsha is attempting to live out in her work what we've been calling throughout this book romantic/pragmatic rhetoric. She has designed her teaching approach as both a response to the world she has experienced and to the study she's made of theories and practices of literacy and learning. It's not coincidental that Freire and Kenneth Burke find an overt place in this writing course. These writers have given to Marsha grounding for her own beliefs as well as methods to translate those beliefs into actions. If one wishes to change violence in a culture, to reduce it, to act against it, one has to understand it. Freire helps Marsha and her students investigate how power relates to violence, how oppression creates it. Burke gives Marsha and her students a blueprint for making decisions about motives for violence, how the act of violence connects to the cultural scene that produces it, how the agent of violence and the purpose of violence are linked.

She has insisted that her own and her students' work have consequences for them and for her, and she has made those consequences conscious for her students through the kinds of assignments the class takes on, the kinds of discussions they hold, the dynamic of student/ teacher interactions they engage in. The personal ethic Marsha holds, philosophically grounded in the dissertation she's written and by writers like Mary Rose O'Reilly, becomes public discussion and community agenda as students use their own beliefs and backgrounds to inform their writing on topics they've chosen to explore, from stances they've decided on and with purposes they make clear to themselves. The writing and discussion are transformed individually and socially by the groups in the class, who've taken responsibility for reading and comment, and who, by the amount and character of their discussion, help individuals articulate, challenge, and assert their own positions.

Marsha's class embodies the attitudes of the host of writers we've been describing here. And it's remade at every meeting, with new discussion, new group endeavor, new strategies, and new knowledge providing the context for the work. It is a classroom guided by belief and tested in experiment.

TEACHERS AS AGENTS OF CONSCIOUSNESS AND BELIEF

The making of a pragmatist I: Patricia Williams's rage and love

Lawyers are labeled as notorious pragmatists in the expedient, cynical sense of the term. To investigate and manipulate in order to find what convinces, what works, what wins—these are the public conceptions of a lawyer's goals and methods. For Patricia Williams, a New York University law professor, that kind of pragmatism prevents the law from doing its real work. Her book, *The Alchemy of Race and Rights,* explores the ethics of her profession and of American society in general. It's a book about teaching and learning, about theory and practice; it's a book about learning to be a romantic pragmatist and to practice romantic/pragmatic rhetoric.

Much of this book is personal, an account of Williams's struggle with schooling, professional discourse, legal systems, and with an inequitable society. As a woman and an African American, she is familiar in deeply personal ways with many of those inequities. She describes the course she teaches in Contracts where she attempts to discuss the ethics of property law. She uses her own history and experience as cases, and she hopes to demonstrate how those experiences connect to community standards and ethical law. Her students are discomfited. She uses descriptions of people sleeping in the subway, of tenements and slumlords, of advertising, to make points about the theory and practice of law. One story she relates to the class is about seeing a child with his parents, pointing to a dog he was afraid of while they insisted to him that the large slathering wolfhound that scared him was "really" no different than the tiny Pekinese who walked on the other side of the street. Williams uses the story as an analogy, "because I think it illustrates the paradigm of thought by which children are taught not to see what they see; by which blacks are reassured that there is no real inequality in the world, just their own bad dreams; and by which women are taught not to experience what they experience, in deference to men's ways of knowing" (1991, 13). The story provokes a confused response among her students, who signed up for the course expecting to experience "that crisp, refreshing, clear-headed sensation that thinking like a lawyer purportedly endows." They dislike the thought of linking women and dogs to academic subjects, and they are "paralyzed by the idea that property might have a gender and that gender might be a matter of words" (13).

But, Williams admits, "I haven't been able to straighten things out for them because I'm confused too" (14). Her book is a path for finding her way out of the confusion that places public and private in such conflict and in such need of one another. The law students complain to the dean: "They are not learning real law, they say, and they want someone else to give them remedial classes. How will they ever pass the bar with subway stories?" (28). Students have a hard time with a teacher who insists that the personal and public merge, that ethical questions are social ones, that the study of contracts and how to be a lawyer is not divorced from the study of culture and individual responsibility to it. They don't want to hear what unsettles.

Much of the book is about Williams's decisions as a writer as well as a teacher. Her writing focuses her work in the classroom and she discovers that the issues of public and personal are much the same in writing academic discourse as they are in deciding how to reach students in class. At one point, Williams delivers a paper on Contract and Community at a National Bar Association meeting and uses the story of her great-great-grandmother, a slave, whose bill of sale to a Tennessee lawyer her family keeps among their papers. The talk includes the discussion of slave and slaveholder, "the control he had over her body. The force he was in her life, in the shape of my life today." The response is warm, but "a friend of mine tells me that in the men's room he heard some of them laughing disparagingly: All this emotional stuff just leaves me cold" (19). But writing, like teaching, involves the whole self for Williams: "I leave no part of myself out, for that is how much I want readers to connect with me" (92).

Williams's honest look at the difficulties of teaching law becomes for all teachers an account of the struggles to behave ethically and responsibly in teaching and learning. It is a book about how the personal matters within the public sphere, of how the "romantic" notion of self must engage with the "pragmatic" notion of the experiential as a method for achieving both real communication and real knowledge. Williams echoes West's analysis of why pragmatism is such an apt response to current contexts: "I think the personal has fallen into disrepute as sloppy because we have lost the courage and the vocabulary to describe it in the face of the enormous social pressure to 'keep it to ourselves'—but this is where our most idealistic and our deadliest politics are lodged, and are revealed" (93). Williams holds on to the personal, insists that her students, who will administer and make laws that will someday affect the personal lives of members of their communities, understand that connection. Her account is a story of progress, not Darwinian, but contingent and experimental.

The making of a pragmatist II: Thomas Riddle:
Putting theory and practice to work together

A graduate student in a teaching practice seminar, Thomas had little experience teaching, and he was taking the class as someone interested in the classroom, but not sure he wanted to try it himself. His work for much of the term centered on defending traditional methods and structures. He worried that lax ideas about the value of student opinions and the need for excellence, as well as limited expectations on the part of teachers and administrators, might be responsible for diminishing literacy among the young. He wanted "them," those students who pay such little attention to the world of learning being offered them, to change and adopt literate ways. His journals and papers, and much of his group discussion, often challenged theories of process, or group endeavor, of encouragement rather than rigor. Yet his actual classroom experience—as these excerpts from his class journal show—challenges his thinking in rich and provocative ways.

Near the end of the semester, Thomas got a job tutoring in an after-school enrichment program at an area middle school with a high percentage minority enrollment. The students he tutors come from, in his words, "the bottom of the barrel." One thirteen-year-old boy already has a daughter and may be dealing marijuana. One girl is pregnant; another might be. Most of the eight students have expressed a desire to drop out of school as soon as they can. They are the kind of students, in short, that Thomas has worried over in his journal entries and group talk. Thomas writes of his experience after meeting with the students twice:

> I'm thinking about the ways I'm interacting with the kids, ways that seem fairly natural and which feel right or good, and I'm realizing that my practice is in significant ways at odds with my theory. We spend so much time encouraging the kids, trying to reward them for good participation, and we're so respectfully polite when disciplining them, that I wonder what happened to my theory?! A kind of pragmatism seems to take over.

Thomas discovers that his practice, which, as he admits, is in conflict with his earlier statements based on an ideological belief and past experience as a student, reaps benefits.

> This sort of thinking seems to have paid off—Monday, our third class, was *great*. . . . We talked about why they were in this after-school program and what they thought that meant about them. . . . We even talked about smoking, using the occasion to have an oration contest. ("Who can give the best justification for smoking to the class?") Some of them really surprised us with their ability to speak; one boy actually gave a little pro and con treatment to the subject, and we loved that, too—talked about how one really good way to persuade people to your way of thinking is to show that you've taken

pro and con into consideration—voila! A miniature introduction to rhetoric!

This mini-lesson illustrates how Thomas learns from these students to use context to provoke new knowledge, how his own position as a teacher is strengthened, not undermined, by his overt discussion with them about the conditions of their academic and social lives. He finds them "smart," full of abilities that he would not have suspected or believed unless he had heard them speak and read and argue. He learns firsthand the importance of a multicultural perspective for students whose own background or ethnicity they have never seen represented in school tasks: "I had them reading from Baldwin's essay 'If Black English Isn't a Language . . .' which sprang from an earlier discussion of vocabulary I didn't know, and their reading ability really impressed me." He learns to move from one topic to another based on what happens in the class, on what students are reading and discussing: "The way things segue into one another is fascinating. But it's whatever seems best *in the moment* that carries the day." Thomas remains concerned about how his theoretical beliefs and his practices clash, and about what that clash might mean for him as a teacher. "I accept the paradox for now," he concludes.

Thomas is on his way to doing as Freire suggests, learning how to make practice the continual test for theory, the element that teachers must circle back to again and again, realizing that theory is developed through practice and that practice is always influenced and altered by theoretical reflection. He is honestly looking at his work as teacher and thinker and beginning the process of "educating his hope," rescuing his belief in students and in himself. It is hard for him not to see this personal, loving practice as "pandering," a word he uses in his journal more than once, but he realizes that for this group of students and for himself as their teacher, the practice has passed the pragmatic test: he can answer clearly the question of what difference his approach has made.

The romanticist as teacher: The case of F. O. Matthiessen

F. O. Matthiessen was more than the author of one of the most influential books ever written on romanticism in American culture. He was also a teacher who transferred his scholarly assessments of the personal, social and transcendental in the work of Emerson, Thoreau, and other major nineteenth-century American writers to his own teaching practices at Harvard in the thirties and forties. Leo Marx, one of Matthiessen's students, devotes a chapter to Matthiessen's teaching in his book *The Pilot and the Passenger* (1988). Titled "The Teacher," this essay shows how Matthiessen took the words he wrote about Emerson and the North American romantics seriously enough to try to make them a part of how he viewed his calling.

The chapter begins with Marx's description of Matthiessen's American literature class, a class Marx has taken a friend to visit with him. This class, and Matthiessen's words about teaching in general, argue for a romantic/pragmatic method of teaching. First of all, as Marx's story demonstrates, Matthiessen made students powerful in the classroom. He treated a class of undergraduates as he would any audience of mature people capable of coming to grips with controversial ideas: "In the course of the hour he referred, with what seemed to my friend a humility rare in college lecture halls, to something he had learned from 'an authority in this class'—a student who had written an essay on Dreiser" (1988, 221). Matthiessen insisted that students had much to contribute, and he insisted that they do so. His belief in them translated into high expectations, especially the expectation that they would be able to do as Berthoff suggests critical thinkers must always do—to "tolerate chaos" (1981, 71). Some students, those who were, as Marx puts it, the "inveterate note scribblers who wanted the material carefully packaged and delivered with neat epigrams were dissatisfied. Too much was left up in the air" (1988, 234). As Freire and others have shown, students don't always, or even usually, react well to being given authority in a classroom.

Yet Matthiessen persisted. He met with students in small tutorial groups, believing that these conferences were the "last bulwark against standardization in a large university" (230). Like Deborah Meier, Matthiessen believed that the smaller the group, the more opportunity for real learning and real responsibility to develop. He made himself ready to learn, especially in these sessions where the lines of discussion might develop in unpredictable ways. Marx says, "There was every reason to expect that either the student or his tutor might be forced beyond his depth during the conference" (235). For many teachers, the prospect of getting "beyond their depth" is a supremely frightening one, especially if it were to happen in the presence of a student. For Matthiessen, it was a "desirable stimulus to creative thinking" (235).

"He was a great teacher," Marx says, "because he taught unstintingly out of himself" (238). Knowing, like Williams, that a teacher must use the whole self to teach, Matthiessen let students see his political stances, let them know what he thought of what he read and why. He believed that a teacher must provide a demonstration of the whole person thinking. And although he knew that everything he believed he could not put into practice, still he realized that good teaching is all about using, rather than hiding, experience for both his students and himself. And like Williams as well, Matthiessen saw his writing and teaching as deeply connected: "Everything that Matthiessen wrote was part of his lifelong project of discovering what he himself believed" (238). Unlike most academic writing, therefore, his work conveys a strong sense of passionate involvement.

The connection between theory and practice, between teaching and learning, between private and public, energized Matthiessen's work. His "reception to dialectical modes of thought," as Marx puts it, his ability to experiment, his need to realize the interpenetration of the individual life and the life of the community, all express his romantic ideology and his pragmatic action (239). It's interesting that most of the scholarly world knows about Matthiessen's romanticism only insofar as he explains the romanticism of the great nineteenth-century writers; Matthiessen's teaching shows that he lived it as well.

Of course, the writer Matthiessen looked to as the most influential of the romantics was Emerson. Emerson saw his essays and speeches as teaching, and teaching of a profoundly spiritual kind. In a journal entry in 1839, Emerson writes of the connection between speaker and hearer in the lecture hall:

> Here is all the true orator will ask, for here is a convertible audience, and here are no stiff conventions that prescribe a method, a style, a limited quotation of books and an exact respect to certain books, persons, or opinions. No, here everything is admissible, philosophy, ethics, divinity, criticism, poetry, humor, mimicry, anecdotes, jokes, ventriloquism, all the breadth and versatility of the most liberal conversation; highest, lowest, personal, local topics. All are permitted, and all may be combined in one speech—it is a panharmonicon. Here is a pulpit that makes other pulpits tame and

ineffectual—with their cold, mechanical preparation for a delivery the most decorous—fine things, pretty things, wise things, but no arrows, no axes, no nectar, no growling, no transpiercing, no loving, no enchantment. (1960–82, 7:165)

Matthiessen quotes this passage in *The American Renaissance* to demonstrate the hope Emerson had for his work, for his speaking and writing, which was for him always about the hope for teaching. And Emerson's hope for teaching, and for all these other romantic/pragmatic rhetoricians, is that students take on the responsibility for learning themselves, become, as Emerson put it, "man thinking." As Emerson critic Stephen Whicher writes, "The best part of Emerson's [program] is, it breeds the giant that destroys itself. Who wants to be any man's mere follower? lurks behind every page. No teacher ever taught, that has so provided for his pupil's setting up independently" (1953, 86). And Harold Bloom echoes that sentiment in his comment that power comes from being freed from the constraints of power in the "already said," the traditional, the known. "Emerson's gnosis of rhetoric wars against every philosophy of rhetoric. Emerson also then is a teacher and a text that must pass away if you or I receive the Newness" (1985, 115).

An undergraduate studying to become a teacher writes about her experience with Emerson's "American Scholar" this way:

> Next semester I will be responsible for what one hundred and fifty students learn in their high school English classes. I do not know exactly where or even what part of English I will be teaching, but I do know how I want to teach. Students will be looking to me for information, and I won't give it to them. Well maybe I'll give them a few historical facts and a little general information, but the bulk of the learning must be done by them. It helps no one for me to tell the students what I think they need to know. I will offer the agenda of course work, and they will experience literature. —Beth

Beth has clearly made what she has read and experienced her own, remade it so that her own students can remake it for themselves.

All the romantic pragmatists we've outlined here, teachers and students and writers, are engaged in the process of becoming conscious of the connectedness of all human enterprises. The realization that one must bring what one has already into any learning situation and that the learning situation depends on what one brings is a perception that links matters of content and style, of writing and reading, of in school and out of school, of teaching and learning, in new and revolutionary ways. "How to join sentences in paragraphs was the same riddle for Emerson as how to reconcile the individual with society," Matthiessen notes (1941, 66). The connection requires the same act of mind—the same act of imagination.

How to Change the Course of the Stream

For all romantic/pragmatic thinkers, whether in the classroom or working outside it, the aim is to create, through writing, teaching and talk, strategies for sustained and practical action. bell hooks is a cultural critic and feminist theorist who has written powerfully about how gender, class and race intersect. The critique she offers argues for the need for all theories to connect to experience, to make feminism and race and class studies connect with lives of people. As a feminist theorist, she criticizes feminist theory that bears no relation to the lives of real women. "Where can we find a feminist theory," she asks, "that is directed toward helping individuals integrate feminist thinking and practice into daily life? What feminist theory, for example, is directed toward assisting women who live in sexist households in their efforts to bring about feminist change?" (1994, 70). hooks makes this perception of the need to make beliefs into actions the touchstone for her recent book on teaching, which is an eloquent reflection on her own development as a thinker and teacher and the way that development connects to theoretical positions and to the development of other teachers' lives. As she says near the beginning of *Teaching to Transgress*, "Despite the contemporary focus on multiculturalism in our society, particularly in education, there is not nearly enough practical discussion of ways classroom settings can be transformed so that the learning experience is inclusive" (35). Teachers, she argues, must be ready to change their teaching styles if they are to honor their own beliefs about accommodating diversity and variety in their classrooms. They must act on belief or, as C. S. Peirce would have said, they must behave pragmatically.

Teaching to Transgress tells the story of how the liberatory teaching practice hooks has learned to value works in the several college classrooms where hooks has taught. She describes the considerable use she makes of Freire by engaging in a mythical dialogue with him, and she considers the virtues of real dialogue by describing the way her thinking and writing have been challenged by published conversations she has written with Cornel West and others. Most of all, this account of teaching is determined by hooks's belief in the possibilities of consciousness. The process of becoming conscious is necessary, as she shows, and painful:

> Again and again, it was necessary to remind everyone that no education is politically neutral. Emphasizing that a white male professor in an English department who teaches only work by "great white men" is making a political decision, we had to work consistently against and through the overwhelming will on the part of folks to deny the politics of racism, sexism, heterosexism, and so forth that inform how and what we teach. We found again and again that almost everyone, especially the old guard, were more disturbed by the overt recognition of the role our political perspectives play in shaping pedagogy than by their passive acceptance of ways of teaching and learning that reflect biases, particularly a white supremacist standpoint. (37)

Teaching to Transgress is a manual of sorts, a narrative that becomes a plan of action for other teachers determined to create equitable spaces for themselves and their students within their classrooms. It's also a hopeful message about the power of thought and language to effect change in actions, a demonstration of how experience and ethical belief can help teachers engage in dialogue with others who may not share many of their beliefs. The rhetorical stance in the book is not unlike Frederick Douglass's, a personal account that becomes a call to action.

Geneva Smitherman, a teacher and linguist whose work has done much to help teachers of English recognize the value of students' own language and the value of collaboration and connection in classrooms, calls this kind of action "changing the course of the stream": "Certainly it is easier," she says, "to work on fitting people into the mainstream than to try to change the course of the stream" (1977, 219). But as she demonstrates how intimately language and consciousness are bound together and argues eloquently for Black English and dialect speech as markers of the kind of consciousness that romantic/

pragmatic thinkers suggest can provoke reflective action, she shows how much the stream must be changed:

> The real concern and question should be, "how can I use what the kids already know to move them to what they need to know?" This question presumes that you genuinely accept as viable the language and culture the child has acquired by the time he or she comes to school. This being the case, it follows that you allow the child to use that language to express himself or herself, not only to interact with their peers in the classroom, but with you, the teacher, as well. (219)

Smitherman and hooks, and the host of others we've described in this book, give us hope that not only can teachers more effectively fit people into a "mainstream" but they can find ways to look up and outside their classrooms to critique the stream itself, a stream of unconsciousness. Operating in that stream, teachers can do little more than "teach to the test," whatever the test happens to be. Becoming aware that methods and systems are contingent and fallible because they are delivered by human agencies, teachers can teach to their students' needs, their communities' beliefs, and their own understandings.

Toward a Pedagogy of Love

> Hope is an orientation of the spirit, an orientation of the heart; it transcends the world that is immediately experienced. . . . Its deepest roots are in the transcendental, just as the roots of human responsibility are. . . . Hope in this deep and powerful sense is an ability to work for something because it is good, not just because it stands a chance to succeed.
>
> —Václav Havel, *Disturbing the Peace*

Freire's recent *Pedagogy of Hope* is in many ways a distillation or an abstract of all his work, for even in *Pedagogy of the Oppressed*, which this book revisits, Freire is guided by a vision of literacy that is profoundly—and methodologically—hopeful. It's this understanding of hope as real, not simply unearned desire or vague wish, that makes Freire's work so important to teachers and students who would change their practices and challenge their theories. The development of the culture circle, the group of learners and thinkers who make their own knowledge by relating and testing their own narratives, is only one of a host of ways that Freire shows his belief in the possibilities of consciousness and of real change. In detailing the process of his growth in understanding, what he's learned since the early days of writing *Pedagogy of the Oppressed*, Freire gives voice to the many teachers and writers who have sustained hope in spite of theories that mock it, or systems that abuse it, and have refused cynicism or despair. "In seeking for deepest 'why' of my pain," Freire says, " I was educating my hope. I never expected things just to 'be that way.' I worked on things, on facts, on my will. I *invented* the concrete hope in which, one day, I would see myself delivered from my depression" (1994, 29).

Why is it important, given all these contemporary stories of the hopeful pragmatist at work, to recognize the links that connect her to a past of romantic thought and pragmatic philosophy in this country? When teachers are able to name their own beliefs, they are able to act on them effectively and confidently. Chris is a first year graduate student and teaching assistant in Hepsie's department. His final project for his first semester theory/practice seminar in teaching was an exploration of fear in the writing classroom, fear that prevents or constrains many teachers from acting on the philosophical beliefs they hold about learning: process, group work, journals, expression, collaboration. It became something more than a theoretical discussion; it became an exploration of love and hope as principled methods for teaching literacy.

The paper begins with an analysis of first-year writing students' fears of using the metaphors they choose to describe their attitudes about writing and writing classes. It continues by creating an essential link between students and teachers: examining a teacher's fears using his own journal and his own experience as a new teacher. "I would argue that the fear circulating in writing classrooms derives not only from students, but also, in varying degrees, from teachers. I'm not referring simply to first-day jitters or anxieties about returning a poor set of essays. I'm talking here about a pervasive, destructive fear that acts as a barrier to a pedagogy based on trust, commitment, and love."

As he writes, Chris notes that "fear nearly keeps me from writing 'love' here (is there some other word that will do?). Fear of being perceived as too soft, too romantic. Fear of being decidedly 'uncool' and utterly dismissable in the current academic climate. Fear even of being somehow untrue to my own affinity to the big cold ideas of critical theory and antifoundationalism." Chris learns from reflecting on his own writing and actions in and out of the classroom. He investigates his own and his students' fears, writes about them, problematizes them, and transforms them into methods for actions based on newly grounded beliefs. "If there is a lesson in this backward glance, it is this: fear can prevent us from loving. . . . I now see that maintaining high standards and holding students responsible for their work and for reaching their potential *is a crucial part of loving them*." Chris has accomplished the romantic/pragmatic act of seeing critical thinking as a matter of responsibility and love, and he's learned how deeply his teaching is a matter of belief.

We've spent a lot of time investigating the work of theorists and practitioners in a variety of settings and time periods in order to demonstrate how romantic/pragmatic rhetoric works in and out of the classroom. We should close this book, we think, by looking at the work of students who've been encouraged to be romantic/pragmatic rhetoricians themselves, invested in their own writing as a part of their own lives and able to put their own beliefs and hopes to the test of real practice. These students are high school juniors, in an urban school in California where the enrollment is more than 50 percent poor and nonwhite. They are part of a new program, called Pacesetter, designed to offer support and challenges to students from a much wider spectrum than traditional "advanced placement" or honors courses have done. It's clear from their powerful responses that these students have come to understand the power of words, of language, for effect. They are becoming critical, engaged thinkers, people capable of acting on their worlds. It's also clear what can happen when a pedagogy gives students a reason to believe that they have something of value to offer as they write.

The writing task was to write "home talk" and "school talk" to reflect some truth about learning and education. For home talk, students transcribed dialogue or a story told to them by someone in their community, using dialect speech and spelling variation to get across the sound. The school assignment asked students to describe their class or friends. It was revised by a group, and it required writers to be conscious of how experience and the narrative were used to describe the class. In other words, it asked students to consider the demands of academic prose. Here is "School Talk," by Laura:

But we know stuff. We don't feel diluted or watered down, vacant or corrupted. We read for pleasure, write with care, think, express judgments, know approximately how long it takes a star's light to reach us and believe that such a trip is extraordinary. Mai Li knows by heart most of Li Po's poems, and some W. H. Auden and all the nursery rhymes from her childhood. Kahlil can tell you about superconductors and quarks. Jacob could solve binomial equations when he was ten. Steve plays trumpet like Wynton Marsalis. Marshall knows why it's profitable to look at Winslow Homer's sea paintings before and after reading Stephen Crane's 'The Open Boat.' Keisha's glad to know Telemachus; I'll read another Jane Austen novel now I know *Pride and Prejudice,* and Danette will read anything by Alice Walker.

We don't do all these things in common. What we have in common is watching Star Trek reruns and loving Spike Lee. We can sneak into Oakland A's games because Marshall's uncle is a ticket taker. . . . We are a motley crew, but for the most part are honest, quick to laugh at ourselves, and value some expressive voice that we might someday own.

Now, "Home Talk," by Benjamin:

Th: Hey, brudda. How come you got such good grade   huh?
Bj: Nah, nah uncle. My grades not that good.
Th: You betcha, good. Jes kidding, man. I know you smart. You got da brain, no lie. And you use it too. It not jes restin gainst da bone. When you was a kid, you kinda screw round, and junior high, everthing was football, football. Now in high school, you got serious. And dat's good. But I worry somtime your serious ways get between you and your friends because they still screw ups, you know. Well, not totally, but not school boys. You know what I mean? Is dat trouble?
Bj: No, Uncle Thaddeus. Don't wory. Sam and Wiliam, we're still good friends. They're serious too. They know they won't be in high school all their lives. We've talked about the future. They know what they have to do to make it. Just sometimes they'd rather party . . .
Th: That's jesit. You got all your life to party. You party too much, you miss da train. Can't afford to miss da train cuz it don't come by too often.
Bj: We're not goin to miss the train. Don't worry.
Th: Jes make sure when it come, you all packed and ready to go and you not sleepin on the tracks like some fool.

Bj: I'll be packed. Don't worry.
Th: You betcha.

Even here at the end of the twentieth century, the train remains a powerful metaphor, an image of change and growth and at the same time a symbol of the forces that can crush, sweep aside, or swallow the settled, inattentive, and the docile. But, as Benjamin has Uncle Thaddeus develop it, the train is also a metaphor for restless, reflective action, for making theory responsible for its consequences, and for the kind of progress that challenges students and teachers to educate their hope and ours.

Works Cited

Abrams, M. H. 1953. *The Mirror and the Lamp: Romantic Theory and the Critical Tradition.* New York: Oxford University Press.

Adams, Henry. 1961. *The Education of Henry Adams: An Autobiography.* Boston: Houghton Mifflin.

Allen, Paula Gunn, and Patricia Clarke Smith.1997. *As Long as the Rivers Flow: Stories of Great Native Americans.* New York: Scholastic Press.

Aristotle. 1954. *Rhetoric.* Translated by W. Rhys Roberts. In *The Rhetoric and Poetics of Aristotle,* edited by Friedrich Solmsen. New York: Modern Library.

Aronowitz, Stanley. 1987. "Postmodernism and Politics." *Social Text* 18:99–115.

Atwell, Nancie. 1987. *In the Middle: Writing, Reading, and Learning with Adolescents.* Portsmouth, N.H.: Heinemann.

Bagley, William. 1907. *Classroom Management.* New York: Macmillan.

Baker, Carlos. 1996. *Emerson Among the Eccentrics: A Group Portrait.* New York: Viking.

Banta, Martha. 1993. *Taylored Lives: Narrative Productions in the Age of Taylor, Veblen, and Ford.* Chicago: University of Chicago Press.

Bartholomae, David. 1995. "Writing with Teachers: A Conversation with Peter Elbow." *College Composition and Communication* 46:62–71.

Bay Psalm Book: Selections. 1975. Brooklyn, N.Y.: Institute for Studies in American Music/City University of New York.

Bercovitch, Sacvan. 1975. *The Puritan Origins of the American Self.* New Haven: Yale University Press.

———. 1985. "Emerson the Prophet: Romanticism, Puritanism, and Auto-American Biography." In *Ralph Waldo Emerson,* edited by Harold Bloom, 29–44. New York: Chelsea House.

Berlin, James. 1984. *Writing Instruction in Nineteenth-Century American Colleges*. Carbondale: Southern Illinois University Press.

———. 1987. *Rhetoric and Reality: Writing Instruction in American Colleges, 1900–1985*. Carbondale: Southern Illinois University Press.

———. 1988. "Rhetoric and Ideology in the Writing Class." *College English* 50:477–94.

Berthoff, Ann E. 1981. *The Making of Meaning*. Portsmouth, N.H.: Boynton/Cook.

———. 1982. *Forming/Thinking/Writing: The Composing Imagination*. Portsmouth, N.H.: Boynton/Cook.

———. 1984. "Is Teaching Still Possible?" *College English* 46:743–55.

———. 1991. "Rhetoric as Hermeneutic." *College Composition and Communication* 42:279–86.

Bizzell, Patricia, and Bruce Herzberg, eds. 1990. *The Rhetorical Tradition: Readings from Classical Times to the Present*. Boston: Bedford Books of St. Martin's Press.

Blanchard, Paula. 1987. *Margaret Fuller: From Transcendentalism to Revolution*. Reading, Mass.: Addison Wesley.

Bloom, Harold. 1985. "Emerson, the American Religion." In *Ralph Waldo Emerson*, edited by Harold Bloom, 97–122. New York: Chelsea House.

Boorstin, Daniel J. 1958. *The Americans: The Colonial Experience*. New York: Random House.

Bradford, William. 1990. *Of Plimouth Plantation*. In vol. 1 of *Heath Anthology of American Literature*, edited by Paul Lauter, 211–33. Lexington, Mass.: D. C. Heath.

Brodkey, Linda. 1987a. "Modernism and the Scene(s) of Writing." *College English* 49:396–418.

———. 1987b. "Writing Ethnographic Narratives." *Written Communication* 4:25–50.

Burke, Kenneth. 1935. *A Grammar of Motives*. Berkeley: University of California Press.

Byers, Thomas B. 1995. "Terminating the Postmodern: Masculinity and Pomophobia." *Modern Fiction Studies* 41:5–33.

Calkins, Lucy. 1991. *Living Between the Lines*. Portsmouth, N.H.: Heinemann.

Callahan, Raymond. 1962. *Education and the Cult of Efficiency: A Study of the Social Forces that have Shaped the Administration of the Public Schools*. Chicago: University of Chicago Press.

Carroll, Michael. 1991. "Comment and Response." *College English* 53:599–601.

Cohen, Morris, ed. 1924. *The Pragmatism of Charles Sanders Peirce and John Dewey.* Boston: Houghton-Mifflin.

Coleridge, Samuel Taylor. 1959. *Biographia Literaria.* In *Major British Writers,* edited by G. B. Harrison, 133–41. New York: Harcourt Brace.

Commager, Henry Steele. 1950. *The American Mind.* New Haven: Yale University Press.

Cooper, James Fenimore. 1912. *The Prairie.* New York: G. P. Putnams' Sons.

Darwin, Charles. 1989. *On the Origin of Species.* 1859. Reprint, London: John Murray.

Dead Poets Society. 1989. Directed by Peter Weir.

de Tocqueville, Alexis. 1945. *Democracy in America.* New York: Vintage Books.

———. 1960. *Journey to America.* Edited by J. P. Mayer. New Haven: Yale University Press.

Dewey, John. 1907. "Education as Engineering." *New Republic* 32:90–94.

———. 1924. Afterword to *Chance, Love, and Logic,* by Charles Peirce, edited by Morris Cohen. Boston: Houghton-Mifflin.

———. 1925. *Experience and Nature.* Chicago: Open Court.

———. 1934. *A Common Faith.* New Haven: Yale University Press.

———. 1976a. *The Child and the Curriculum.* 1902. Reprinted in vol. 2 of *The Middle Works, 1899–1924,* edited by Jo Ann Boydston, 271–93. Carbondale: Southern Illinois University Press.

———. 1976b. "Psychology and Social Practice." 1899. Reprinted in vol. 1 of *The Middle Works, 1899–1924,* edited by Jo Ann Boydston, 131–51. Carbondale: Southern Illinois University Press.

———. 1976c. *School and Society.* 1899. Reprinted in vol. 1 of *The Middle Works, 1899–1924,* edited by Jo Ann Boydston, 1–240. Carbondale: Southern Illinois University Press.

———. 1980. "Democracy in Education." 1916. Reprinted in vol. 9 of *The Middle Works, 1899–1924,* edited by Jo Ann Boydston, 1–356. Carbondale: Southern Illinois University Press.

———. 1981. *The Dewey School.* 1936. Reprinted in vol. 11 of *The Later Works, 1925–1953,* edited by Jo Ann Boydston, 191–217. Carbondale: Southern Illinois University Press.

———. 1982. "Philosophy and Democracy." 1918. Reprinted in vol. 11 of *The Middle Works, 1899–1924,* edited by Jo Ann Boydston, 41–54. Carbondale: Southern Illinois University Press.

———. 1984a. "The Development of American Pragmatism." 1925. Reprinted in vol. 2 of *The Later Works, 1925–1953,* edited by Jo Ann Boydston, 3–21. Carbondale: Southern Illinois University Press.

———. 1984b. *The Public and Its Problems*. 1946. Reprinted in vol. 2 of *The Later Works, 1925–1953,* edited by Jo Ann Boydston, 235–373. Carbondale: Southern Illinois University Press.

———. 1984c. *The Sources of a Science of Education*. 1929. Reprinted in vol. 5 of *The Later Works, 1925–1953,* edited by Jo Ann Boydston, 1–40. Carbondale: Southern Illinois University Press.

———. 1987. "Art as Experience." 1934. Reprinted in vol. 10 of *The Later Works, 1925–1953,* edited by Jo Ann Boydston, 1–353. Carbondale: Southern Illinois University Press.

———. 1988. *Experience and Education*. 1938. Reprinted in vol. 13 of *The Later Works, 1925–1953,* edited by Jo Ann Boydston, 1–62. Carbondale: Southern Illinois University Press.

Dickenson, Donna. Introduction to *"Woman in the Nineteenth Century" and Other Writings,* by Margaret Fuller. Oxford: Oxford University Press, 1994.

Dickinson, Emily. 1961. *Final Harvest*. Boston: Little, Brown.

Diggins, John Patrick. 1994. *The Promise of Pragmatism: Modernism and the Crisis of Knowledge and Authority*. Chicago: University of Chicago Press.

Douglass, Frederick. 1963. *Narrative of the Life of Frederick Douglass: An American Slave*. New York: Dolphin Books.

DuBuisson, David. 1993. "Can our Public Schools Ever be Liberated from the Curse of Self-Esteem?" *Greensboro News and Record,* 23 March.

Elbow, Peter. 1986. *Embracing Contraries: Explorations in Learning and Teaching*. New York: Oxford University Press.

———. 1995. "Being a Writer vs. Being an Academic: A Conflict in Goals." *College Composition and Communication* 46:72–83.

Elbow, Peter, and Pat Belanoff. 1989. *Sharing and Responding*. New York: Random House.

Emerson, Ralph Waldo. 1903. "The Young American." In *Nature: Addresses and Lectures,* 362–81. Ralph Waldo Emerson Centenary Edition. Boston: Houghton Mifflin.

———. 1960–82. *The Journals and Miscellaneous Notebooks of Ralph Waldo Emerson*. Edited by William H. Gilman et. al. 16 vols. Cambridge: Harvard University Press.

———. 1969a. "The American Scholar." In *Selected Prose and Poetry,* edited by Reginal Cook, 39–55. New York: Holt Rinehart.

———. 1969b. "The Poet." In *Selected Prose and Poetry,* edited by Reginal Cook, 121–40. New York: Holt Rinehart.

———. 1969c. "Self-Reliance." In *Selected Prose and Poetry,* edited by Reginal Cook, 72–93. New York: Holt Rinehart.

————. 1985. *Nature: A Facsimile of the First Edition*. Boston: Beacon Press.

Emig, Janet. 1971. *The Composing Processes of Twelfth Graders*. Research Report No. 13. Urbana: National Council of Teachers of English.

————. 1980. "The Tacit Tradition: The Inevitability of a Multi-Disciplinary Approach to Writing Research." In *Reinventing the Rhetorical Tradition*, edited by Aviva Freedman and Ian Pringle, 9–17. Ottawa: Canadian Council of Teachers of English.

"Exhibit at the National Academy of Design." 1988. In *The Railroad in American Art*, edited by Leo Marx and Susan Danby, 95. Boston: MIT Press. Originally published in *Knickerbocker*, July 1853.

Faigley, Lester. 1986. "Competing Theories of Process: A Critique and a Proposal." *College English* 48:527–42.

Fish, Stanley. 1989. *Doing What Comes Naturally: Change, Rhetoric, and the Practice of Theory in Literary and Legal Studies*. Durham, N.C.: Duke University Press.

Flower, Linda, and John Hayes. 1979. "Writer-Based Prose and Reader-Based Prose: A Cognitive Basis for Solving Problems in Writing." *College English* 41:19–39.

Franco, Jean. 1987. "Gender, Death and Resistance: Facing the Ethical Vacuum." *Chicago Review* 35:59–79.

Franklin, Benjamin. 1935. *Poor Richard's Almanac*. Philadelphia: David McKay.

————. 1983. *The Autobiography and Other Writings*. New York: Dodd, Mead.

————. 1990. "Information to Those Who Would Remove to America." In vol. 1 of *Heath Anthology of American Literature*, edited by Paul Lauter, 810–13. Lexington, Mass.: D. C. Heath.

Freire, Paulo. 1970. *Pedagogy of the Oppressed*. New York: Continuum.

————. 1985. *The Politics of Education*. South Hadley, Mass.: Bergin and Garvey.

————. 1990. *Education for Critical Consciousness*. New York: Continuum.

————. 1994. *Pedagogy of Hope: Reliving Pedagogy of the Oppressed*. New York: Continuum.

Freire, Paulo, and Donaldo Macedo. 1987. *Literacy: Reading the Word and the World*. South Hadley, Mass.: Bergin and Garvey.

Frye, Northrop. 1957. *Anatomy of Criticism*. Princeton: Princeton University Press.

Fuller, Margaret. 1994. *"Woman in the Nineteenth Century" and Other Writings*. Edited by Donna Dickenson. Oxford: Oxford University Press.

Garrison, William Lloyd. 1963. Preface to *Narrative of the Life of Frederick Douglass: An American Slave*. New York: Dolphin Books.

Gere, Anne Ruggles. 1987. *Writing Groups: History, Theory, and Implications*. Urbana: Southern Illinois University Press.

Gilbreth, Frank B., and Lillian Gilbreth. 1924. "Classifying the Elements of Work." *Management and Administration* 8 (August): 151–54.

Gould, Stephen J. 1989. *Wonderful Life: The Burgess Shale and the Nature of History.* New York: W. W. Norton.

———. 1995. "Ladders and Cones: Constraining Evolution by Canonical Icons." In *Hidden Histories of Science,* edited by Robert B. Silvers, 37–67. New York: New York Review.

Gradin, Sherrie. 1995. *Romancing Rhetorics: Social Expressivist Perspectives on the Teaching of Writing.* Portsmouth, N.H.: Boyton/Cook, Heinemann.

Griffin, Susan. 1995. *The Eros of Everyday Life.* New York: Doubleday.

Hairston, Maxine. 1982. "The Winds of Change: Thomas Kuhn and the Revolution in the Teaching of Writing." *College Composition and Communication* 33:76–88.

Halloran, S. Michael. 1982. "Rhetoric in the American College Curriculum: The Decline of Public Discourse." *Pre/Text* 3:245–69.

Havel, Vaclav. 1990. *Disturbing the Peace: A Conversation with Karel Hvizdala.* Translated by Paul Wilson. New York: Knopf.

Hawthorne, Nathaniel. 1962. *The Scarlet Letter.* Edited by Sculley Bradley, Richmond Croom, and E. Hudson Long. New York: W. W. Norton.

———. 1967. *The House of the Seven Gables.* Edited by Seymour Gross. New York: W. W. Norton.

Herrnstein-Smith, Barbara. 1988. *Contingencies of Value: Alternative Perspectives for Critical Theory.* Cambridge: Harvard University Press.

Holy Bible. N.d. King James Version. Cleveland, Ohio: World Publishing Company.

hooks, bell. 1994. *Teaching to Transgress: Education as the Practice of Freedom.* New York: Routledge.

Hutcheon, Linda. 1988. *A Poetics of Postmodernism: History, Theory, and Fiction.* New York: Routledge.

Irving, Washington. 1899. *Rip Van Winkle.* New York: G. P. Putnam's Sons.

James, William. 1912. *The Will to Believe and Other Essays in Popular Philosophy.* New York: Longmans, Green.

———. 1960. "The Ph.D. Octopus." In *Writings, 1902–1910,* 1111–19. New York: Library of America.

———. 1969. "Philosophical Conceptions and Practical Results." 1920. Reprinted in *Collected Essays and Reviews,* 406–37. New York: Russell and Russell.

———. 1975. *Pragmatism (1907) and The Meaning of Truth (1909).* Cambridge: Harvard University Press.

————. 1978. "The Pragmatic Method." 1898. Reprinted in *The Works of William James: Essays in Philosophy*, 123–39. Cambridge: Harvard University Press.

Kinneavy, James. 1971. *A Theory of Discourse*. Englewood Cliffs, N.J.: Prentice-Hall.

Knoblauch, C. H., and Lil Brannon. 1984. *Rhetorical Traditions and the Teaching of Writing*. Upper Montclair, N.J.: Boynton/Cook.

Kozol, Jonathan. 1991. *Savage Inequalities: Children in America's Schools*. New York: Crown.

————. 1995a. *Amazing Grace: The Lives of Children and the Conscience of a Nation*. New York: Crown.

————. 1995b. "Spare Us the Cheap Grace." *Time*, 11 December, 96.

Kuhn, Thomas. 1970. *The Structure of Scientific Revolutions*. Chicago: University of Chicago Press.

Kuklick, Bruce. 1977. *The Rise of American Philosophy: Cambridge, Massachusetts, 1860–1930*. New Haven: Yale University Press.

Lauer, Janice, and William Asher. 1988. *Composition Research: Empirical Designs*. New York: Oxford University Press.

Lerner, Gerda. 1997. *Why History Matters: Life and Thought*. New York: Oxford University Press.

MacDonald, Heather. 1995. "Why Johnny Can't Write." *The Public Interest* 120:3 (11).

McGowan, John. 1991. *Postmodernism and Its Critics*. Ithaca: Cornell University Press.

Marx, Leo. 1988. *The Pilot and the Passenger: Essays on Literature, Technology and Culture in the United States*. New York: Oxford University Press.

Marx, Leo, and Susan Danly, eds. 1988. *The Railroad in American Art*. Boston: MIT Press.

Mather, Cotton. 1990. *Magnalia Christi Americana*. 1702. Reprinted in vol. 1 of *Heath Anthology of American Literature*, edited by Paul Lauter, 401–21. Lexington, Mass.: D. C. Heath.

Matthiessen, F. O. 1941. *The American Renaissance*. New York: Oxford University Press.

Meier, Deborah. 1995. *The Power of Their Ideas: Lessons for America from a Small School in Harlem*. Boston: Beacon.

Mill, John Stuart. 1967. "What is Poetry?" In *Literary Essays*, edited by Edward Alexander. Indianapolis, Ind.: Bobbs-Merrill.

Miller, Perry. 1973. "From Edwards to Emerson." In *American Transcendentalism: An Anthology of Criticism*, edited by Brian Barbour, 63–82. South Bend, Ind.: Notre Dame University Press.

Miller, Susan. 1995. "The Death of the Teacher." *Composition Forum* 6:42–52.

Murphy, James, ed. 1982. *Rhetorical Tradition and Modern Writing.* New York: Modern Languages Association.

Murray, Donald. 1985. *A Writer Teaches Writing.* Boston: Houghton Mifflin.

National Education Association. 1901. *Addresses and Proceedings of the Annual Meeting, 1901.* Washington, D.C.: NEA.

———. 1913. *Addresses and Proceedings of the Annual Meeting, 1913.* Washington, D.C.: NEA.

The New England Primer: A Reprint of the Earliest Known Edition. 1899. Edited by Paul Leicester Ford. New York: Dodd, Mead.

Newkirk, Thomas. 1991. "Politics of Composition Research: The Conspiracy Against Experience." In *The Politics of Writing Instruction: Postsecondary,* edited by Charles Schuster, R. Bullock, and J. Trimbur, 119–35. Portsmouth, N.H.: Heinemann.

North, Stephen. 1984. "The Idea of a Writing Center." *College English* 46: 433–46.

———. 1987. *The Making of Knowledge in Composition: Portrait of an Emerging Field.* Upper Montclair, N.J.: Boynton/Cook.

———. 1994. "Revisiting 'The Idea of a Writing Center.'" *Writing Center Journal* 15:7–19.

O'Reilly, Mary Rose. 1993. *The Peaceable Classroom.* Portsmouth, N.H.: Boyton/ Cook, Heinemann.

Pacesetter English. 1996. *Voice of Modern Cultures,* 113-14. Princeton, N.J.: College Entrance Examination Board and Educational Testing Service.

Peirce, Charles Sanders. 1924. *Chance, Love, and Logic.* Edited by Morris Cohen. Boston: Houghton Mifflin.

———. 1931–58. *Collected Papers of Charles Sanders Peirce.* Edited by Charles Hartshorn and Paul Weiss. 16 vols. Cambridge: Harvard University Press.

———. 1958. *Selected Writings: Values in a Universe of Chance.* Edited by Philip J. Wiener. New York: Dover.

———. 1992. "How To Make Our Ideas Clear." In *The Essential Peirce: Selected Philosophical Writings,* edited by Nathan Hauser and Christian Kloeser, 124–41. Bloomington: Indiana University Press.

Reynolds, David. 1988. *Beneath the American Renaissance: The Subversive Imagination in the Age of Emerson and Melville.* New York: Knopf.

Rorty, Richard. 1989. *Contingency, Irony, and Solidarity.* Cambridge: Cambridge University Press.

———. 1991. *Objectivity, Relativism, and Truth.* Cambridge: Cambridge University Press.

Rose, Mike. 1985. "The Language of Exclusion: Writing Instruction at the University." *College English* 47:341–59.

———. 1995. *Possible Lives: The Promise of Public Education in America*. Boston: Houghton Mifflin.

Rowlandson, Mary. 1990. *Narrative of the Captivity and Restoration of Mrs. Mary Rowlandson*. In vol. 1 of *Heath Anthology of American Literature*, edited by Paul Lauter, 318–42. Lexington, Mass.: D. C. Heath.

Russell, David. 1988. "Romantics on Writing: Liberal Culture and the Abolition of Composition Courses." *Rhetoric Review* 6:132–51.

Schwartz, Robert. 1988. "Whatever Happened to Pragmatism?" In *Values and Value Theory in Twentieth-Century America: Essays in Honor of Elizabeth Berg*, edited by Murray G. Murphey and Ivar Berg, 37–45. Philadelphia: Temple University Press.

Smitherman, Geneva. 1977. *Talkin' and Testifyin': The Language of Black America*. Boston: Houghton Mifflin.

Spellmeyer, Kurt. 1996. "After Theory: From Textuality to Attunement with the World." *College English* 58:893–913.

Spencer, Herbert. 1915. *Works*. New York: Appleton.

Springsteen, Bruce. 1986. "Reason to Believe." On *Bruce Springsteen and the E Street Band Live, 1975–1985*. Columbia Records, C5X 40558 C 40561 BL 40561.

Taylor, Frederick. 1919. *Shop Management*. New York: Harper and Brothers.

———. 1947. *The Principles of Scientific Management*. New York: Harper and Row.

Thoreau, Henry David. 1966. *Walden and Civil Disobedience*. Edited by Owen Thomas. New York: W. W. Norton.

Ticknor, Caroline. 1913. *Hawthorne and His Publisher*. Boston: Houghton Mifflin.

Tompkins, Jane. 1990. "Pedagogy of the Distressed." *College English* 52:653–60.

———. 1991. "Comment and Response." *College English* 53:601–5.

Ulrich, Laurel Thatcher. 1982. *Good Wives: Image and Reality in the Lives of Women in Northern New England (1650–1750)*. New York: Knopf.

Vygotsky, Lev. 1962. *Thought and Language*. Edited and translated by Eugenia Hanfmann and Gertrude Vakar. Cambridge: MIT Press.

West, Cornel. 1989. *The American Evasion of Philosophy: A Genealogy of Pragmatism*. Madison: University of Wisconsin Press.

———. 1993a. *Keeping Faith: Philosophy and Race in America*. New York: Routledge.

———. 1993b. *Prophetic Thought in Postmodern Times. Beyond Eurocentrism and Multiculturalism: Volume 1*. Monroe, Me.: Common Courage Press.

Westbrook, Robert B. 1991. *John Dewey and American Democracy.* Ithaca: Cornell University Press.

Whicher, Stephen. 1953. *Freedom and Fate: An Inner Life of Ralph Waldo Emerson.* Philadelphia: University of Pennsylvania Press.

Whitman, Walt. 1959. "Song of Myself." In *Complete Poetry and Selected Prose.* Boston: Houghton Mifflin.

Will, George. 1996. "Teach Johnny to Write." *Washington Post,* 2 July.

Williams, Patricia. 1991. *The Alchemy of Race and Rights: Diary of a Law Professor.* Cambridge: Harvard University Press.

Wills, Garry. 1990. *Under God: Religion and American Politics.* New York: Simon and Schuster.

Winterowd, W. Ross. 1992. "Where is English—In the Garden or in the Agora?" *Focuses* 5:65–89.

Winterowd, W. Ross, with Jack Blum. 1994. *A Teacher's Introduction to Composition in the Rhetorical Tradition.* Urbana, Ill.: NCTE.

Winthrop, John. 1908. *History of New England, 1630–1649.* Edited by James Kendall Hosmer. New York: C. Scribner's Sons.

Wordsworth, William, with Samuel Taylor Coleridge. 1969. *Lyrical Ballads.* 1798. Reprint, edited by J. B. Owen, London: Oxford University Press.

Zanger, Jules, ed. 1960. *Diary in America.* 1839. Reprint, Bloomington: Indiana University Press.

Index